THE
DRUID'S
LODGE
CONFEDERACY

THE DRUID'S LODGE CONFEDERACY

THE GAMBLERS WHO MADE RACING PAY

PAUL MATHIEU

RACING POST

This edition published in 2015 by Racing Post Books
27 Kingfisher Court, Hambridge Road, Newbury, RG14 5SJ

First published in Great Britain in 1990

10 9 8 7 6 5 4 3 2 1

A catalogue record for this book is available from the British Library.

ISBN 978–1-910498–11–8

Cover designed by Jay Vincent
Text designed by J Schwartz & Co

Printed and bound in the UK by CPI Group (UK) Ltd, Croydon, CR0 4YY

www.racingpost.com/shop

With thanks to those who've made race-going so enjoyable. From the beginning: Anthony de Freitas and David Hill. During thirty-plus years at the Cheltenham Festival: Ian Dodds-Smith, John Goodacre, Michael Green and Andrew Jones. Between the flags: Peter Grodzinski and Jonathan Neesom. On the annual busman's holiday: Eddie Fremantle.

Contents

Acknowledgements

My thanks to James de Wesselow and Julian Brown of Racing Post Books for suggesting this new edition of *The Druid's Lodge Confederacy*. Thanks also to the racecourse book and art seller Rupert Mackeson, for (his words) "continually whingeing and whining to them" about a reprint, until they gave in. Jay Vincent and John Schwartz have given the book a smart new design and artwork.

A feature of the first edition which attracted friendly comment was its attempt to express late Victorian monetary values in their modern equivalents. Thanks to Sam Williamson of MeasuringWorth for permission to use his firm's retail price tables to update all the pound sterling numbers to 2013.

The book includes comparisons, over a period of more than 100 years of the number of racehorse owners, horses in training, and races run. That's been made possible by data provided by Sally Richards at Weatherbys and Rodney Pettinga at Raceform. George McGrath at the National Association of Stable Staff and Lauren Hilton at the Association of British Bookmakers have helped to bring staff pay and bookmaking industry stats up to date. Thanks also to the Racehorse Owners Association.

John Elliot and Giles Ormerod, respectively of the farming and polo side at Druid's Lodge, have brought the estate's story up to the present. My wife Heather has, as always, provided support and infinite tolerance.

My thanks to Hilary Aitchison for the photograph of her great-great-uncle Tommy Lewis. Finally, thanks also go to Michael Fallon, who has provided fresh stories, correspondence and a hitherto unseen family photograph to enhance the book's portrait of his grandfather Jack, the trainer genius of Druid's Lodge.

Author's Note

The sums of money wagered and won by the Confederates have been shrunk by time and inflation.

The original edition of this book was the first racing title which tried to adjust for inflation. The basis of its calculations was that the spending power of £1 in the Confederates' heyday was the equivalent of £48 when the book was published in 1990.

In the period from 1990 and 2015, the pound has continued to erode rapidly. There are various ways to calculate the relative value of sterling between different dates: it can be based on prices, incomes, or general economic output. The MeasuringWorth website has explanations of the many variables. Its UK retail price index (RPI) table suggests that to match the spending power of £1 (or a £1 bet) in 1895, one would've needed to spend £100.80 in 2013.

Therefore, the numbers in the book for prize money, bets, winnings and wages can be conveniently multiplied by 100 to give their broad equivalent today. Of course, nothing's that simple: even in the two decades covered by this book, the spending power of sterling fell by 15 per cent. So here and there, for emphasis, the inflation-adjusted 2013 figures are given in italics.

In centuries to come when Druid's Lodge stands on lonely Salisbury Plain a ruin, a sister to its neighbour Stonehenge, which has ever been a mass of mystery, it will doubtless be pointed out as an historic monument in connection with the story of the Turf.

The guide, as he takes tourists over the spot in an aeroplane, will point out Stonehenge as mysterious, and the ruins of Druid's Lodge as more mysterious still. Doubtless, he will add that it was a famous place, not a philanthropic institution, but once known as Druid's Lodge.

But what further explanation may be offered and what adjectives brought into play in describing those ruins is a matter too far ahead for us to conjecture. One thing the Salisbury Plain showman may megaphone to his load in the sky, namely, that 'Christmas Daisy won the Cambridgeshire twice in succession, ladies and gentlemen, the second time so easily that Mr Cunliffe might have ridden it himself'.

Robert Sievier, *The Winning Post*, 1910.

1.

The Confederates

THE GIANT OWL perches, unblinking, on a branch of the cartoonist's tree. Grasped firmly in his talons is a desperate, wriggling figure: the *Bookie*. Hanging further along the branch is *The Punter Who Interfered*. Sharing the tree with the owl is a jaunty Robin Hood figure: *The Forester*. Below struts a precise little bird with a ski-jump nose and pince-nez. The roots of the tree are inscribed *Druid's Lodge, Fallon* and *Ypsilanti*.

Even without the identification of Druid's Lodge, readers of the 28 October 1905 issue of *The Winning Post* had no difficulty in identifying the cartoon's subjects. The illustrator Starr Wood – 'The Snark' – had produced lively caricatures of some of the best-known racing personalities of the time. The monumental, impassive owl was a City financier, Percy Cunliffe. The nose and the pince-nez belonged to an Irish stud-owner and West End impresario, Wilfred Purefoy. *The Forester* was a celebrated huntsman, Frank Forester. The roots of their enterprise were an isolated, purpose-built racing stable on Salisbury Plain – Druid's Lodge – and a brilliant trainer, Jack Fallon. Ypsilanti was the first of many big-race winners that Cunliffe,

Purefoy, Forester and their friends Edward Wigan and Holmer Peard sent out from Druid's Lodge.

At the start of this century, the five had the bookmakers by the throat as no stable before or since, and as no stable ever will again. So secretive was the management of their racing affairs that they were nicknamed by one racing journalist, 'The Hermits of Salisbury Plain'. More generally, using the name for what we now call a syndicate, Cunliffe, Purefoy and the others were known as the Druid's Lodge Confederacy.

Percy Cunliffe came from a family with extensive City interests. His brother Walter, Baron Cunliffe, was Governor of the Bank of England. Cunliffe owned land on Salisbury Plain, and derived a considerable income from renting it to the Army for manoeuvres. He speculated successfully in the South African goldfields. The Eton-educated Cunliffe was a huge man, well over six feet and upwards of twenty stones. To his irritation, his friend Wilfred Purefoy persuaded his tailor that since so much more cloth was needed to cover Cunliffe, his suits should cost him extra. In fact Cunliffe rarely showed irritation, or indeed any other emotion. He was quietly sardonic, but an accumulator of the good things of life. The pride of his silver collection was a large two-handled cup made by the most sought-after of English silversmiths, Paul Lamerie. It was bad luck that when Cunliffe gave Lamerie's name to a horse, the animal turned out to be useless. Cunliffe also had a fabulous collection of portrait miniatures on loan to the Victoria and Albert museum – and, it was said, a fabulous collection of pretty young girls. He was a director and shareholder of Sandown Park, and a steward at Brighton.

Wilfred Bagwell Purefoy was landed gentry, in the strict sense of an entry in *Burke's*. His family seat was at Greenfields in the west of Tipperary. His father was High Sheriff of the county, his grandfather a dean, his great grandfather the local MP. Purefoy went to Harrow, then Sandhurst. He was commissioned in a crack cavalry regiment, the 3rd Hussars. He sent in his papers when 27, and stepped into a life of entrepreneurial adventure that earned him the affectionate family nickname of 'Wicked Wilfred.' His friends called him 'Pure.' He was thin, reserved, and had sharp grey eyes; his appearance suggested an accountant or banker, his background indicated rural respectability. In fact, Pure was restless, bohemian and cosmopolitan. He loved Greenfields. In its greenhouses he collected rare orchids and water-lilies. On the estate he bred cattle, established a large racing stud – and even improved the local donkey breed by importing an expensive moke from Egypt. He travelled widely and frequently: to America, to Africa, to India, and to wherever a salmon rose to a fly. He had rooms in Jermyn Street in the West End. In short, he enjoyed an expensive lifestyle. To finance it, he threw himself with demonic energy into various business interests.

Purefoy joined in the exodus of fortune-seekers to South Africa in the 1880s. He met Percy Cunliffe in the Transvaal but unlike Cunliffe, he made no profit from his visit. Subsequent attempts to join gold syndicates were unsuccessful. In London, he invested in the best-known restaurant of the time, Romano's in the Strand, and in two of the major music-hall theatres, the Gaiety and the Adelphi. He kept a close eye on Broadway for potential hits. On one visit to New York, spying $2 tickets to a show selling for $10 and $12, he acquired the London rights. It was an instant success. He befriended American stars and brought them to the Gaiety. Purefoy was a director of the Autostrop Safety Razor company, a shareholder and director of Kempton Park, and a serious player in the stock market.

Frank Forester was one of the best-known horsemen of his day. He was born within a view-halloo of the Quorn kennels in Leicestershire, went to Eton, and like Purefoy was commissioned in the 3rd Hussars. He was a great-nephew of the last Duke of

Cleveland, and came into a large inheritance when the Duke died in 1891. Some of the inheritance – Battle Abbey and the Wrington Vale estates in Somerset – he sold at once. Other estates in and around Bath were entail, and provided him with a large rental income. All his long life, Forester used his wealth to finance his passion for hunting and racing, and also his generosity towards good causes, notably the building of hospitals in Bath and London. A stern disciplinarian at the races (he was a steward at Bath and Croxton Park) and in the hunting field, Forester had been high-spirited in his youth. One escapade had him up before the magistrates' bench in Manchester in 1887 for commandeering a private cab on his way to a ball, 'furious driving' and drunken and incapable behaviour. Among his companions – giving a false name to the police – was Purefoy. Forester was warned 'that he would not be allowed in Manchester to run away with cabs,' and fined a guinea. He rode in steeplechases before breaking a thigh in a fall at Punchestown in 1890. He continued to ride on the flat right up to the War, partnering his own horse Denis Auburn to victory in the Private Sweepstake at Croxton Park in 1912 and 1913, and again – to a rapturous reception from the crowd – at the age of 54 in 1914.

But Frank Forester was a huntsman first and foremost. He rode to hounds with the Hussars in Yorkshire and in Ireland, where he revived the disbanded Clonmel Harriers. He was the Old Berkshire's MFH before being offered the Mastership of the Quorn in 1905. He led that distinguished pack for 13 seasons, and was recalled with relish in Colin Ellis's *Leicestershire and the Quorn Hunt* as a 'rather terrifying man in the early stages of a run.'

> He did not attempt either to stop his horse or to take any
> fence slowly. Utterly fearless, he rode his steeplechasers across
> High Leicestershire at a pace that astonished the hardest

Quornite. The fences were his and his horse's business, and it was the business of the field to keep out of his way. He is remembered as a silent man at the meet but vociferous in the field, flying across country and shouting as he went.

But they all say he did hunt the country most awfully well! There was no nonsense during the cub-hunting season about having an agreeable ride round and a coffee-housing party.

Even in the big covers, the proportion of cubs that he meant to kill were killed. The remainder – and any old foxes that did not know it already – learned that a cover was not a good place to stay in when Captain Forester was about. When the full season started the foxes went away across country as if the devil were after them – and Captain Forester's hounds came out at the sound of his voice like a pack of devils to a sorcerer's summons.

Edward Wigan was a small, uncommunicative man. When Arthur Sarl of *The People* described him as 'One of the shrewdest men on the Turf with whom I have ever come into contact,' he added 'though of quiet and reserved demeanour.' It was an understatement. It was said of Purefoy that if he'd been asked how many legs did one of the Druid's Lodge horses possess, he'd have referred the questioner to his trainer. Yet Purefoy seemed positively garrulous alongside Wigan, who was so little known that in more than one memoir he's described as an Irish vet, though he was an English businessman.

Wigan came from a wealthy family of hop merchants. He went to Eton and to Cambridge. He wasn't academic. His master at Eton complained that 'he only pays enough attention to turn what I've said into a Spoonerism.' At Cambridge he was noted for keeping horses and for extravagance. But he was a first-rate sportsman at racquets and polo, and also an exceptional shot. By his mid-twenties,

Wigan had come into a vast fortune, with an income running into tens of thousands a year. In so far as he had a public personality, it was as a pioneering breeder of Aberdeen Angus cattle, and as a shrewd financier. Horsemanship, great wealth and a dislike of publicity: Wigan's attributes and personality made him another perfect partner for Cunliffe's enterprise.

If Wigan was no Irish vet, Holmer Peard certainly was – the best around, and a stud manager and racing administrator too. Peard first made his name as the successful manager of the Cork Park racecourse. He was then invited by a group of investors, including Purefoy, to manage the planning, design and construction of the Phoenix Park course. When it opened in 1902 he was its first secretary. Cunliffe and Purefoy were major shareholders. Holmer Peard was also the pre-eminent racehorse vet of his time. He was sent for by Royalty to treat their sick horses, he was reckoned an unequalled judge of a yearling, and twice he was at the cusp of racing history.

First when the colourful gambler, sometime bookmaker and all-time rogue and litigant Robert Sievier asked him to look over the draft of yearlings sent up to Newmarket sales in 1900 by the Duke of Westminster. Sievier particularly wanted Peard's opinion of a grand-looking bay filly by the Prince of Wales's 1896 Derby winner Persimmon out of Ornament, a full sister to the unbeaten 1886 Triple Crown winner Ormonde. Peard could hardly contain his enthusiasm. As the bidding mounted towards the then unheard-of level of 10,000 guineas (£1,058,000), Peard urged Sievier to buy her. And buy her he did. The successful bid stood as a record for almost 20 years, but since the filly was Sceptre, she was cheap at the price. Under Sievier's somewhat erratic management (she often ran to land a gamble to pay off his more pressing debts), and later when he took over her training himself, Sceptre won four classics and four other races. Sievier's critics said that in more conventional ownership she would never have been beaten: a carping verdict on a career that included victory in the 1,000 Guineas, 2,000 Guineas, Oaks and St Leger.

Ten years after his decisive influence on Sceptre's purchase, Peard was looking over some foals at the Straffan Station Stud in Kildare with their breeder, Edward Kennedy. Peard was much taken with an oddly-marked grey colt by the staying handicapper Roi Herode. A price of £800 had been agreed when Kennedy asked Peard what did he intend to do with the colt? 'Why,' replied Peard, 'cut him, and put him by to make a great jumper.' 'In that case,' retorted Kennedy, 'the deal's off. I won't sell him to you.' Some jumper. The colt, out of Vahren, grew – uncut – to be one of the greatest juvenile sprinters in the history of English racing: The Tetrarch. Sold at Doncaster in 1912 for £1,430 to Atty Persse, who passed him on to his cousin Major Dermot McCalmont, The Tetrarch quickly showed his wily trainer the kind of ability that happens along once in a racing lifetime.

His jockey Steve Donoghue, who described him as 'a sort of elephant grey with big splotches of lime colour,' joked that The Tetrarch must have been a racehorse in a previous incarnation, so quickly did he learn his job. On Persse's gallops at Stockbridge he was 'tried' as big a certainty as ever looked through a bridle. Persse had an ultra-reliable old handicapper to test his two year olds. In one trial The Tetrarch gave the older horse a stone (*61lb* worse than weight for age) and pulverised him. Persse hid away The Tetrarch if visitors came to the yard. When the colt made his debut at Newmarket, the travelling head lad managed to smuggle a few pounds into the racecourse farrier's hand to get the lads' money on, but Persse – who always believed the time to strike was first time up – landed the coup of his life at 5–1.

The Tetrarch was never beaten. He won the Woodcote Stakes at Epsom by three lengths and the Coventry Stakes by 10 lengths. At Sandown, he overcame bad hampering at the start to beat a useful filly, conceding 17lb. Then he won the Rous Memorial by six lengths; the Champion Breeders' Stakes at Derby by four; and finally the Champagne Stakes at Doncaster by three lengths – from a winner of seven previous races. He was backed down to 5–2 to win the 1914 Derby but broke down, and never ran as a three year old. Plenty of good judges thought he would have walked the race. Others, Donoghue included, said he had far too much speed to possess any pretensions of stamina. At stud, The Tetrarch got the 1920 2,000 Guineas winner Tetratema ('No more than a high class sprinter,' says the *History of the English Turf*) and the scintillating but non-staying filly Mumtaz Mahal. To sustain the stamina debate, though, The Tetrarch sired three St Leger winners in five years: Caligula (1920), Polemarch (1921) and Salmon Trout (1924).

Holmer Peard delighted in all this. The more races The Tetrarch won, the more his success at stud, the more relish Peard took in telling of the great jumper that might have been. Peard was a tall, handsome, decisive man. He had a wicked humour but a short temper, and little or no time for anyone not interested or involved in horses. Walking in Cork one day, he startled his companion by pointing out an attractive girl and announcing, 'That's the woman I shall marry.' Luckily, she turned out to be the daughter of a local riding school owner, and marry her he duly did.

2.

On Salisbury Plain

PUREFOY USED TO say that he made his money in London and spent it in Ireland. And in ensuring that there was always plenty in the coffers, his attention was increasingly focused on racing – and on betting. Others had shown the way. The long era of the greatest of all gambling owners, Captain James Machell, was drawing to a close. Lord Carnarvon's Whatcombe stable and Captain Bewicke's Grateley syndicate were two contemporaries who had the bookies running for cover. Purefoy decided that racing could be made to pay, and pay handsomely. He'd acquired a taste for the Turf while racing a few steeplechasers in Germany in the early 1890s. Back at Greenfields, musing with Holmer Peard on the rich pickings available from the London bookmakers, he was on the lookout for a private trainer. He noticed a young man from Roscommon called Jack Fallon.

Jack had impeccable credentials. He was the son of a small-time trainer who sent him to England at the age of thirteen to 'do his two' at the Kingsclere stables of John Porter. On returning to Ireland, Fallon spent some time with Michael Dennehy on the Curragh, rode over fences, and then turned to training. Before long he gave every sign of knowing the exact time of day, and just when he might've been looking for bigger challenges and opportunities, along came Purefoy with an offer to set him up in England with a guaranteed supply of horses to train. In September 1894, Fallon was installed with a mixed string of Purefoy's and Peard's flat and jumps horses at Everleigh, north of Salisbury. The stable – now occupied by Richard Hannon Jr – had been owned by 'The Mate,' Sir John Astley, a celebrated Victorian owner and gambler who was briefly a Member of Parliament. At one public meeting he was asked what he thought of Sir Wilfred Lawson's Liquor Bill. His reply, which deserved to win any election, was 'I don't know much about Sir Wilfred's liquor bill, but mine's a damned sight too high!'

That winter, Purefoy re-met Percy Cunliffe in South Africa. Cunliffe too had been nurturing predatory thoughts about bookmakers. The pair's objective was simple: to part the bookies from their money. The strategy would be to operate private stables, and to spread the costs and risks among a few like-minded friends. Pure had the trainer. He and Cunliffe had the friends. Frank Forester, Edward Wigan and Holmer Peard represented an extraordinary resource: all three were horsemen and one was a top vet. And of the five Confederates, four – all but Peard – were multi-millionaires by today's measure. All five were experienced administrators or businessmen. Their roles would be clear-cut. Cunliffe was to be the master planner, the identifier of targets; Purefoy was the 'racing commissioner,' in charge of stable administration and betting. Peard would judge the gallops on his visits from Ireland, besides giving unmatched veterinary advice; Forester and Wigan would add counsel and finance.

One aspect was undecided: location. Cunliffe had the answer. His and Purefoy's scheme necessitated privacy. What could be more private than Salisbury Plain? And as it happened, high up on the Plain, Cunliffe owned a property with potential, just two miles

south-west of Stonehenge. It was historic terrain for the training
and racing of horses. A little to the north of Stonehenge, running for
almost two miles east to west is the 300-feet wide *cursus*, or course,
dating back 4,500 years. Its eighteenth-century discoverer William
Stukeley imagined the *cursus* 'Crowded with chariots and horsemen,'
and hailed it as 'certainly the finest piece of ground that can be
imagined for the purpose of a horse race.'

The grass of Salisbury Plain, wrote Stukeley, 'composes the softest
and most verdant turf in the world, extremely easy to walk on and
[rising] with a spring under one's feet.' When Cunliffe talked to
Wilfred Purefoy about his plans for a stable, he had an obvious
starting-point. It was a coaching inn called the Druid's Head. It
stood in isolation on the downs, not far south-west of Stonehenge on
the Salisbury road. The nearest hamlets were a couple of miles away,
at Middle Woodford and Berwick St James. In the middle of the
nineteenth century, the Druid's Head had been a noted training yard,
run by Isaac Woolcott with the help of his brother Harry. They were
nick-named 'Guts and Gaiters.' Harry was generously proportioned,
Isaac a formal dresser. Their horses were stabled behind the pub, and
galloped on the downs opposite.

On a fine October Wednesday morning in 1895, Jack Fallon
walked 16 of Purefoy's string the few miles from Everleigh to their
new home at the Druid's Head stables. Cunliffe had closed the pub.
He began the construction of an imposing house, Druid's Lodge, a
hundred yards back from the road on the open downs. A veranda ran
round three sides of the new house, to allow Cunliffe and his guests
to enjoy the views across the Plain. A few yards from the Lodge,
Cunliffe built a large U-shaped stable block. The stables were the
last word in luxury and attention to detail. They contained individual
boxes for 40 horses in training, each box lined with metal strips to
discourage crib-biting. All the woodwork was oak. The boxes were

enclosed, with a covered passage-way running along the front of the doors. This arrangement meant warmth in winter and coolness in summer – not to mention security.

The tack-room, dominated by a beautiful coaching-clock taken from the Druid's Head, had a wood-block floor that wouldn't have disgraced a ballroom. By the tack-room was a kitchen where the lads' meals were prepared. Stairs led up to a dormitory for the lads and apprentices. The dormitory was the entire loft of one leg of the U. In another loft was an elaborate feed-milling machine. A large coal-fired sauna allowed rugged-up horses to be sweated, to speed up conditioning. Besides retaining a few of the loose boxes from the Woolcotts' days, to house the hacks and horses out of training, Cunliffe built a block of eight hospital boxes a little way away from the main stables. They made it possible to isolate any coughs or runny noses. They served also as a quarantine area for horses new to the yard. Nothing was left to chance.

Between building the Lodge and the stable block and turning some cottages into homes for Fallon and the married lads, Cunliffe sank the best part of *five million pounds* into Druid's Lodge. Now, the trees and shrubs that he planted have grown to maturity and the Lodge and the stables are hidden from the road. Then, the buildings stood gaunt and exposed on the downs. Any resemblance to a penal institution was intentional. Fallon's former master John Porter used to complain of the unsolicited letters that his lads received. He quoted one:

> Sir, I now venture to ask if you are agreeable to correspond
> with me for the racing season. You may rest assured it would
> be quite safe, and it will be kept quite secret between us. If you
> should favour me by answering, you could name a place where
> you could get your letters safe.

Very likely, Jack himself received similar missives. He described Druid's Lodge as like 'a fortress in the Sahara':

> Life amid the unending sands couldn't have been more
> lonely than the existence we led on Salisbury Plain. There
> was absolutely nowhere to go. The sight of a horse and trap
> coming along the road brought all the stable lads to the gates
> with their eyes popping with curiosity.

Cunliffe and Purefoy were thoroughly alert to the temptations facing low-paid lads. They took every precaution possible. The lads' mail was opened to see who they were writing to, and who was writing to them. A strict curfew was enforced at night. All the staff were locked into their dormitory. The iron concertina gate that barred their exit is now at the National Horseracing Museum in Newmarket.

Occasionally, of course, information leaked. Fallon was down at the hospital boxes when he 'suddenly smelt a most beautiful aroma.' Thinking for a moment that he must be in 'a fashionable restaurant instead of a racing stable,' he took a deep sniff – then ordered the lad in charge of the box to turn out his pockets. First appeared a silk handkerchief, drenched in scent. Then a gold fob watch and chain. The lad was rolling in money. He admitted helping himself to the stable's winners. It didn't suit Cunliffe and Purefoy one bit. If each of the 50 or 60 staff employed at Druid's Lodge by the end of the 1890s had his own coterie of punters, what pickings would be left for the Confederates? At the same time, it would have been inconsistent – not to say hypocritical – to expect the lads to be indifferent to betting when the whole *raison d'être* of the stable was plundering the bookies. Purefoy had the answer. If any of the lads wanted to back a stable runner, that was fine, but they had to place their bets through him. Winnings and losses would be credited or debited with their wages.

In an establishment run along the lines of Druid's Lodge, it was always possible that things weren't what they seemed. The horse burning up the gallops might not be intended to win; in races with ante-post betting, it might not even be running. But Purefoy could hardly reveal intimate stable plans when a lad tugged his forelock and asked for '10 shillings on my horse next week, Sir.' Instead, Pure maintained a charming subterfuge. If a lad had his bet on a horse that wasn't 'intended' or didn't run, Pure wouldn't deduct the loss from his pay. With a straight face he told his crestfallen employee that – wasn't it just as well? – he hadn't been able to find a bookmaker.

Cunliffe was a remote, unsmiling figure. They said he was terrified of horses, but he wanted to maintain appearances by riding up to the gallops on a hack. So the lads had standing instructions, whenever he was due down from London, to gallop a broad-backed old cob to the point of exhaustion. By the time the enormous Cunliffe was perched on its back, the poor creature scarcely had the energy to put one foot in front of another, still less give him any trouble.

Purefoy was the best sort of paternalist employer. Back at Greenfields, he paid for every medical and dental expense for his staff. He had a kind word for every stable lad, and a genuine interest in their welfare. Many of the Druid's Lodge lads were brought over from Tipperary, and they were a raw-boned lot. The sophisticated locals delighted in teaching them to spell: 'd-o-g spells cat,' and so on.

Cunliffe used to fret about the Irish lads' visits to confession. On high days and holidays they were taken to mass in Salisbury. Other times, the Catholic priest would visit the stable. Cunliffe asked Fallon if it was possible that the lads might be owning up to more than they should in the confessional box? And if so, could Jack have a quiet word in Father's ear? Another reverend, Parson Twining from Middle Woodford, worried about the welfare of the lads in their isolation. He organised football matches and other games. Cunliffe gave Fallon £100 to donate to parish funds. On another occasion, Cunliffe learned that Salisbury hospital, where any injured lads from the yard were taken, didn't have a lift, so he paid for one to be installed. And more than once he arranged jobs for unhealthy lads in the friendlier climate of South Africa, and paid for their travel.

The lads were easy meat for the permanent staff at Druid's Lodge. The gallops man, Pearce, with a couple of helpers and a stone jug of beer perched on his shoulder, filled every hole, trapped every mole, and strung chicken-wire alongside the gallops to keep the rabbits at bay. He kept himself to himself, but the cook and the chauffeur enjoyed useful second incomes at the lads' expense. Food was regular, but hardly plentiful: bread and butter at breakfast, some meat with potatoes and greens at lunch, and the lads had to fend for themselves in the evening. The cook always had a bread-and-butter pudding in the oven – at a penny a portion for a hungry lad. The estate farm usually had an egg to spare, but the cook would charge another penny to boil or fry it. Cunliffe's chauffeur came more expensive: when his master wasn't expected, he'd gladly run a car-load of lads down to Salisbury for the evening at sixpence each. And that was sixpence out of a weekly wage of 10 shillings for the stable lads, three shillings for the young apprentices. Sixpence for an excursion, though, was good value for the lads, whose constant companion was boredom. They were up before seven o'clock, riding out first lot before breakfast, then second lot. Then they mucked out, and whisked their horses with tightly-wound spirals of straw, rubbed vigorously down the horses' shoulders and quarters to muscle them up. Whisking, along with sweating the horses in the sauna, was a short cut to conditioning them to full fitness. After lunch, the lads were free till evening stables. When all the horses had been set fair and the curfew descended, there was no entertainment apart from card games, boxing and bullying the youngsters. The action at the card table centred on a three-card game called German Banker.

As for bullying, the younger lads and new apprentices were routine targets. Charles Gianella, who arrived at Druid's Lodge as a boy of 14 in 1909, recalled being thrown up onto a table and told to 'Sing, yer bastard!' Being stronger-willed than most, he refused: 'Excuse me, I know exactly who my parents are!' and was subjected to a painful beating. Stripped, he had his ankles tied to lunging reins thrown over the beams of the dormitory ceiling. Hanging upside down, he was spun in a circle while his tormentors beat his backside with riding crops and sprigs of holly. When he still refused to sing, he was upended over the stable cesspit. Eventually, Gianella's spirit won the day, and the bullies moved on to easier victims. Well into his nineties, though, he insisted that the lads' life at Druid's Lodge was no worse than at other local stables, and far better than at many. The lads' lot at Druid's Lodge was hard, but not harsh. There wasn't the routine cruelty of some of the stables of the time.

Gianella represented the under-class in Cunliffe's enterprise: the apprentices. Apart from Bernard Dillon, a talented young rider who was imported from Tralee by Purefoy in 1901, the apprentices were mostly just gallops fodder. They did the work of the lads at less than half the lads' pay. Gianella was in the majority who spent their time at Druid's Lodge, in his case five years, without ever getting a ride in public. The apprentices did, however, have plenty to do on the gallops. The stable's isolation, the opening of the lads' post, and the locking-up at night all represented severe obstacles for the professional touts of the time. But the precautions surrounding the gallops elevated secrecy to an art form.

Rarely were the newspaper touts any great nuisance to the Confederates. They used to appear on their bicycles, doff their caps respectfully to Cunliffe, and be sent on their way with a generous present. As a result, newspaper gallops reports tended towards 'Fallon's string all did easy work' generalities when Druid's Lodge was reviewed. More than once, Cunliffe's mordant humour was satisfied by having a horse reported as 'doing excellent work' when it was dead.

Across the road from the stable, a series of wonderful gallops ran parallel to each other in the north-east direction of Stonehenge, reached along a path called the Stonehenge Trail. The furthest gallops were on a stretch of downs called Ashburton's – reputedly won by Cunliffe from Lord Ashburton in a bet. The undulations and extent of Ashburton's allowed Fallon and the gallops staff to recreate the conformation of virtually any racecourse in England when aiming a horse at a specific race. Every yard of the gallops and the surrounding downs was open, exposed, and offered no shelter to a lurking tout. So the trials were impossible to observe from close at hand. Any tout caught snooping by the stable's outriders was sent on his way with a thrashing.

When a serious trial was arranged, work would begin as usual, with half the string saddled up. The apprentices and the work riders were taken to the tack room and weighed out with their backs to the scales. On the Stonehenge Trail, a handful of them would be ordered to swap mounts. Up on the gallops, horses in twos and threes would be sent home, until only those concerned in the trial remained. The lads were then switched around again, until any chance of feeling or guessing what weights were in each horse's weight cloth had been eliminated. Then, with instructions to the riders from Fallon, the trial would take place. At the finish stood Peard, equipped with a fancy chronometer that clocked the time of the first three horses. Peard also acted as judge of the trial. He admitted finding his dual responsibilities nerve-racking. Fallon compiled detailed gallops reports; Cunliffe and Purefoy watched and assessed.

To the lads, all remained mystery. They couldn't know if the horse that finished in front in the trial was really the 'winner,' or if the animal a length or two back in third or fourth was the best at the weights – whatever they'd been. Even if they wanted to tell, the lads couldn't. Fallon knew. Cunliffe and Purefoy knew. Their Confederates knew. But as the stable's first runners were prepared for the start of the flat in 1896, none of them had the slightest intention of disclosing anything that would interfere with their plans.

3.

Prizes, Bets and Dope

CONTINUITY BEING ONE of the charms of racing – whether represented by a classic winner's first crop making their debuts, or an old chaser battling round the gaffs for the umpteenth year – it's no surprise to find that in the 1890s and 1900s, the season's first feature race was the Lincoln, its last the November handicap. In between were the same five classics. Among the leading owners were Lord Derby and the reigning Monarch. The elite jockeys commanded large retainers and big-race winning incentives. *The Sporting Life* provided daily race cards, results, betting summaries and 'Man on the Spot' reports, as the *Racing Post* does today.

The similarities to racing today, however, mask vast differences. Racing was on a smaller scale in 1900. There were only 1,224 owners registered. In 2014, thanks to the growth of syndicate and club ownerships, it was 5,172 – though since a syndicate is recorded as one owner, the number of individuals involved in ownership today is much higher. In 1900, some 3,350 horses ran on the flat in Britain in 1,645 races. In the traditional flat season of 2014 (Doncaster April to Doncaster November), 9,662 individual horses ran in 4,995 races. In summary, the number of owners in 2014 was 323 per cent higher than in 1900; the number of horses who appeared on the racecourse was 288 per cent higher; and the number of races increased 304 per cent. On the face of it, a tripling of races means greater opportunities for prize-money. In fact, most of today's owners are worse off than their equivalents of 1900.

On the plus side, every race now has prize money to third place, and feature races often reward the horses placed fourth and even further back. Thanks to infusions of sponsors' and Levy Board (that is, punters') money, owners don't run for their own stakes to the extent that they did in 1900, and there are far fewer selling races. In 1900, in most races, only the winner took home anything at all. Few races rewarded any finisher outside the first two. Even in the 1,000 and 2,000 Guineas, the owner of the third-placed horse received nothing more than the entry money back.

On the debit side, the lowest prize money today on the flat is less than a third that of 1900. Every race run in England and Scotland that year was worth a minimum £100 (£10,080) to the winner. By contrast, opening the 2014 form book at random, it isn't hard to find meetings where the winning owners took home an average of just over £2,600 per race. At the top end, there isn't quite the same disparity, but the most valuable race of 1900, the Eclipse, was worth 20 per cent more to its winner than the Derby of 2014. Winning prize money of the top 10 conditions races in 1900 was, in real terms, also 20 per cent higher than in the equivalent races of 2014.

If prize money was higher in 1900 than today, so too were training costs, but not because of the labour content. The stable lads' miserable ten shillings [£50] a week in 1900 highlights the progress that's been made in turning employment in a racing yard into a career. Today's senior stable staff earn an agreed minimum of £350 a week, an inexperienced youngster is paid £232 or more a week. Pensions are standard. And win pools are now formalised at three percent of prize money – meaning around £3.5 million to be shared between the UK's 7,600 or so stable staff. There were no pensions or bonus guarantees for their counterparts in 1900.

Colonel Harry McCalmont, who owned Isinglass, winner of the 1893 Triple Crown, reckoned the outgoings of his Newmarket stable, typically with twenty-five horses in training, to be £472 (£47,578) per horse. He listed these training expenses:

25 horses at 50s per week each	3,125
Travelling expenses	500
Heath tax	175
Veterinary surgeon	100
Miscellaneous expenses	300
Yardmen and other help	500
Rent of stables	600
Jockeys' fees	1,000
Jockeys' retainers	1,500
Entries and forfeits	4,000
Total:	**£11,800**

McCalmont didn't reveal his trainer's salary, but it would've brought the per-horse annual cost close to £50,000 a year in our money. Today, the average cost is £22,000, so in real terms ownership is much less expensive. However, the obvious conclusion – that today's owners are better off – is misleading. First, because if the owner who wins a £200,000 first prize is getting 20 per cent less than from the equivalent race in 1990, the lower training costs don't make up the difference. Second, at the lower prize-money levels, returns to the winners have fallen by up to three-quarters. *The Racing Post* could be arguing today, though it was *The Sporting Life* in October 1904, that 'It is perfectly clear that winning one or two races cannot pay without betting.'

Cunliffe's business brain was fully alert to the economic reality – some would say unreality – of racehorse ownership. Unlike Forester and Purefoy, who had horses in training before the Confederacy was formed, and Peard, who in various ways earned his living from the racehorse, Cunliffe had no background in racing. He evaluated Purefoy's proposition like any other business venture, and he saw that the key to making it pay, if it could be made to pay, was successful betting. Very well: he would make the investment, surround himself with the best talent available, and be patient.

Prize money apart, the big-race scene that Cunliffe surveyed was noticeably different in 1900. In what are now the Group or Pattern races the most striking feature is the decline of the Eclipse. Sandown's centrepiece was the most valuable flat race in 1900. In 2014, it wasn't even in the top 10, its worth in real terms having fallen by 73 per cent.

Sponsorship dominates big races and their names nowadays, particularly among the handicaps. There was only a minuscule amount of sponsorship in 1900; the Great Eastern Railway acknowledged its many race-going passengers (equine as well as human) by sponsoring a handicap at Newmarket. Today, among the dozen richest handicaps, only Royal Ascot's Hunt Cup, Wokingham and Britannia are not sponsored. But some of the races that nowadays don't attract much attention were guaranteed, ninety years ago, to whet the appetites of Cunliffe and Purefoy. Among them was the Jubilee. For many years after its inception in 1887 to mark Queen Victoria's 50th year on the throne, it was *the* flat-race handicap. Not surprisingly, the Jubilee was the target chosen by the Confederates for their first major gambles.

Today's punters would consider themselves in seventh heaven if they could be let loose in the betting environment that Purefoy set out so skilfully to exploit. True, their counterparts in 1900 didn't have the facility of walking off the street into a betting shop, choosing a board price or SP about their fancies, and then watching them on a live TV transmission. They also remained in near-total ignorance of what horses were likely to take part in any given event. As at a point-to-point today, racegoers couldn't be sure of the runners until the numbers board was hoisted. And, in the absence of patrol cameras and photo-finishes, stewarding and judging were haphazard. The racegoer of 1900 also had no Tote to bet with as an alternative to the bookmakers. There were no betting exchanges, no mobile devices. But the clever punter had plenty going for him. There was place-only betting. There was no concentration of bookmaking power in a few hands, and no sophisticated communications systems as exist today.

In 2014, 87 per cent of Britain's 9,021 betting shops were owned by the five main bookmaking chains. Each has sensitive antennae to pick up the merest whisper – the cobra's scales on the bathroom tiles – of an intended gamble. Their shops' tills are linked to computer systems at head office, so that bets and liabilities can be monitored in real time. In parallel, the betting exchanges provide a wide-angle perspective on markets' supply and demand, in the process inverting the time-honoured system whereby the on-course betting market dictated the starting prices on which bets were settled. Now, the odds shown on on-course bookmakers' electronic boards change, more or less in sync, in response to moves on the betting exchanges – often without any punters within yards. Back in 1900, consolidation of the bookmaking industry hadn't begun, and there was certainly no mechanisation. The hundreds of individual bookies had no formal communications system. Big gambles could escape detection if spread thinly enough. And there were plenty of small bookmakers willing to lay bets that today's shop managers are obliged to report to head office, for approval to accept them. The communications that did exist were heavily weighted in favour of the punter. The accepted method of getting 'on' was by telegram. Telegraph offices time-stamped every telegram as it was handed in, and then set about transmitting it. Imagine the possibilities. A horse is primed for its race. A string of telegrams are prepared with bets, preceded perhaps by 'blocking' telegrams containing lengthy messages of no consequence. All the telegrams are handed in and timed just before the race.

The SP coup was never better arranged than by Captain Bewicke and his owners at Grateley. It was never better described than by Robert Sievier in *The Winning Post*, after Bewicke and the stockbroker G. A. Prentice had landed a gigantic touch with a two year old called Stratton in a seller at Nottingham:

> A little village was found. A small shop was discovered in it, which had added to its everyday affairs that of a telegraph office. At a given moment a huge bundle of telegrams were handed in, piled on top of one another, to back Stratton, addressed to various bookmakers scattered all over England. Well, how plain it all is! One female telegraphic operator, one instrument, and sheaves of wires! Result? Stratton won at 10–1. The bookmakers were congratulating themselves at not laying the winner, when the wires began to come in, and they continued to pour in till nightfall.

Percy Bewicke was a hard man. In his days as an amateur rider, he used to have his commission agent waiting by the paddock exit, or even on the racecourse, and at the last possible moment on his way to post he would instruct the agent to put £1,000 or more on his mount. Lesser mortals might have found this nerve-racking. But as

Sievier marvelled, it was uncanny how well Bewicke rode on these occasions: 'The horse, the man and the bet appeared as one.' Bewicke, though, never pursued the telegram coup to the lengths of one gang of punters who bought their own post office and set their own times on its telegraph machine. Things went along merrily and profitably until they were discovered.

The Stratton affair hit the books so hard that it spelt the beginning of the end of concerted telegram betting. Bookmakers already had a rule that clients couldn't lend their names to others' telegrams (for the purpose of disguising the true source of a bet), but it was unenforceable. Tattersalls Committee then introduced the twelve o'clock rule, refusing to countenance any telegrams handed in after midday. This rapidly fell in to disrepute when some bookies continued to accept losing bets timed after midday, but instituted all manner of outraged enquiries when a winner or two showed up. It was a welsher's charter for bookie and punter alike, and eventually Tattersalls settled on the compromise that where they found evidence of a concert party, a settling limit of 4–1 could be imposed.

If the betting environment of over a hundred years ago seems like another game altogether, there were two more features of that era which contrast sharply with racing today. In an age where there were fewer races, fewer horses in training, and fewer owners, it appears odd that there were significantly *more* racecourses. No less than 47 courses staged flat racing in 1900, against 32 in 2014. The explanation lay in both the large number of sweepstakes races – where the owners in effect ran for their own money, without the racecourses having to dip into their pockets at all – and in the regional nature of racing, in an era when transport was still dominated by rail.

Nowadays, horses can be whisked speedily from one end of the country to the other, on motorways and in comfortable horseboxes. From Druid's Lodge, there being hardly a trunk road worth the name, every intended runner had to be taken to the railway at Salisbury and put in a special horse carriage, to be sent by train to its race meeting. Some stables were near enough to a station to walk their horses to the train. Druid's Lodge being eight miles from Salisbury, its runners were carried in a Foden's box pulled by two greys. The implications of rail transport for racehorses were simple: stables only had runners at meetings with straightforward train connections. The Confederates never had a runner in Scotland, and apart from a handful of runners at Haydock and a couple of successful long-range pots at Newcastle's Seaton Delaval Stakes, the stable never went north of Liverpool and Derby. Its horses ran and won in the Midlands, in the South and on the metropolitan courses.

An even greater limitation was presented by the possibility that however fit and fancied your horse was, you might none the less run up against a rival who had, quite legitimately, been doped. The problem has mutated over the last hundred years, but not halted. Either side of the Second World War, the Jockey Club presided over an epidemic of doping that made for lurid headlines and tarnished the sport's image. The Club reacted with a blend of incompetence and vindictiveness. Blame for a doped horse was assigned solely to its trainer; a number of lives were ruined while the perpetrators mostly went free. One of the Club's analysts tested suspect substances with her tongue. On such foundations were cases decided. The most notorious doping case concerned Pinturischio, 'got at' twice when ante-post favourite for the 1961 Derby. Fingers were also pointed at the defeats – each horse was favourite and ran tailed off – of Ribiofilio in the 1969 2,000 Guineas and Gorytus in the 1982 Dewhurst Stakes. A nadir was reached when former jockey Dermot Browne ['the Needle Man'] doped 23 horses in two months in 1990. They included the Champagne Stakes favourite Bravefoot, easy in the betting before labouring home last. It'd been attacked with a fast-acting tranquiliser.

The latest instances of drug detection in British racing have included the application or possession of steroids by Gerard Butler, Mahmood Al Zarooni and the Irish trainer Philip Fenton. Most recently, cobalt chloride has been detected in Australia and the USA; it's said to boost horses' endurance. The battle against drugs in athletics, cycling and other sports suggests that racing's regulators will never be able to put up the 'job done' sign.

Back in the early days of Druid's Lodge, the Jockey Club was caught completely unawares.

It had no rule prohibiting dope. So far from hoods with chemistry degrees feeding favourites with potions to slow them down, there was evidence everywhere that powerful stimulants were being administered to make horses run faster. The half-dozen years of the dopers' heyday exactly straddled the turn of the century, and the most skilled practitioners were a group of Americans come to England to escape the reforming zeal of Teddy Roosevelt. They didn't invent doping. A Bishop Auckland vet, Jimmy Deans, used to prepare what the northern fraternity called 'speedy balls' long before the American invasion of the late 1890s. There was nothing covert about the activities of Deans. He advertised his dopes in the *Sportsman* and the *Yorkshire Post* – with the specific claim that he could improve horses' form by 14lb to 21lb. On the racecourse, he was known cheerfully to tip horses to his friends on the grounds that he'd just given them an injection.

Incredibly for the modern-day racegoer, accustomed to trainers being fined hundreds of pounds even when the Jockey Club has accepted that some infinitesimal trace of an illegal substance was an accident, open and blatant doping went on unchallenged and unpunished. Until, that is, the Americans really hit their stride. The five principals were the owners William ('Bet You A Million') Gates and James Drake; the brilliant jockeys Johnny and Lester Reiff –

Lester with weight problems, Johnny a natural lightweight; and a talented trainer, Enoch Wishard. Their chosen dope was cocaine.

The Sporting Luck wrote sarcastically that:

> A desire to imitate the feats of the whirling Dervish, to climb trees, or lie down with the restful, happy expression of a pig in clover, accompanied by heavy sweating and bad attacks of the shakes, is foreign to the well-trained thoroughbred.

'After 1900, this horrible practice increased rapidly,' George Lambton recalled in *Men and Horses I Have Known*, 'and by 1903 it had become a scandal.' At first Lambton doubted that any dope could make a bad horse into a good one, but events rapidly changed his mind. As he put it, very strange things occurred.

> One constantly saw horses who were notorious rogues running and winning as if they were possessed of the devil, with eyes starting out of their heads and the sweat pouring off them. These horses being mostly platers, and running in low-class races, did not attract a very great deal of attention.

That changed when the Americans got hold of a handicapper called Royal Flush. Formerly trained up in Yorkshire, he was sent to the December sales in 1899, and knocked down to James Drake. Royal Flush had won his share of races – including a four-timer in modest races at Carlisle, Manchester, Pontefract and Newcastle. But as a six year old entire, he couldn't be expected to have much improvement in him. He was sold for 450 guineas (just under £48,000). Miracles do happen on the Turf, especially with a powerful stimulant to encourage them. It certainly must have seemed miraculous to his former owner (who ironically became an official handicapper) when, after three 'sighters' for Wishard, Royal Flush ran third in the 1900 Jubilee, a race in which Cunliffe and Purefoy had a huge gamble frustrated by a short head, and followed up by winning the Hunt Cup and £2,490. Brought back to six furlongs for the Stewards' Cup, Royal Flush was sent off favourite and beat eighteen rivals by no less than six lengths. He then carried 9st 7lb to victory in a little handicap at Brighton, before an easy win at Doncaster on St Leger Day. By then Gates and Drake had collected £4,111 in win and place money from Royal Flush, plus anyone's guess in bets – all for an outlay of 450 guineas and a few judicious doses of dope. Their final coup with the horse represented the ultimate racing certainty: a non-trier in a two-horse race.

Wishard had accepted a challenge from the connections of a top sprinter, Eager, to run a match over six furlongs at Hurst Park for £500 a side. On the face of it, there could be only one result. Eager had run close up behind the placed horses in Royal Flush's Stewards Cup, conceding 28lb to the winner. At the level weights of the Hurst Park race he simply had to win. Unless, of course, the dope worked the oracle once more with Royal Flush. It didn't. Instead, the Americans arranged for a few bookmaker confidants to lay Royal Flush for every farthing they could. They themselves backed Eager. And they ran Royal Flush undoped. The betting opened with both horses at 10–11. After £5,500 was laid on Eager to win £5,000, he rapidly shortened to 4–7, while Royal Flush drifted to 2–1. The race was a formality, Morny Cannon on Eager taking a nice lead to half-way before cantering home by three lengths.

The chicanery over Royal Flush was preceded by a more or less identical stroke with the appropriately named Americus at Newmarket a fortnight earlier. Here, though, Drake and Gates had unwelcome attention drawn to them. Robert Sievier, who 'took a strong dislike to these people *en bloc*' had divined that Americus wasn't scheduled to win. The horse was opposed by an evident no-hoper called Sonatura – 27lb worse off with Americus despite finishing behind him a month earlier. Yet the seeming million-to-one-on shot Americus was oddly easy to back. Having established that the Americans hadn't a penny on the favourite, Sievier stood in front of them by the rails of the Jockey Club stand and roared 'Americus does not win, for £5,000. An even £5,000 against Americus.'

There were no takers. Nor could Sievier get a bet of any kind on the 'no-hoper.' Needless to say, the Lester Reiff-ridden Americus was run over by Sonatura. It was a profitable manoeuvre for Reiff, but a risky one. Only half an hour earlier the stewards had carpeted him for finishing out of the first three on the odds-on favourite in a six-runner seller. The stewards 'were not altogether satisfied,' but 'did not consider that the evidence was such as to convince them that the horse had been pulled.' For the first time in my memory,' wrote Sievier, 'there was a general public hooting at Newmarket.' The incident was the beginning of the end for Reiff and his patrons.

The Jockey Club were loath to follow any lead set by Sievier, himself hardly their favourite owner. But from within the Establishment, George Lambton produced damning, conclusive evidence. After a notorious case 'When a horse, after winning a race, dashed madly into a stone wall and killed itself,' Lambton decided something needed to be done. He told the Jockey Club that he intended to experiment with dope, to prove its effect on horses' performance. The results were sensational.

> At that time I had in my stable some of the biggest rogues
> in training. The first I doped was a chestnut gelding called
> Folkestone. [He] had refused to do anything in a trial or race.
> He was always last. I first of all doped him in a trial. He fairly

astonished me, for he jumped off in front and won in a canter.
I sent him to Pontefract, where he beat a field of 14 very easily,
and nearly went round the course a second time before his
jockey could pull him up. He won a race again the next day,
was sold and never won again.

Lambton had six doses left, all administered by bottle. The first five
produced four winners and a second – including a big handicap with
a notorious shirker, who won 'with a stable boy up, like the most
honest horse in the world.' The sixth dose was passed to the Duke of
Devonshire's trainer to perk up another animal that had disappointed
all year. It too won. With Lambton's damning evidence, the Jockey
Club looked at the American set-up, and warned off Lester Reiff
indefinitely. His brother Johnny decamped to Paris, where he rode
with great success. James Drake followed him, and continued his
high-rolling ways there for many years.

In the *Racing Calendar* of 1904, there appeared in the Rules of Racing
for the first time, under Corrupt Practices and Disqualifications, the
warning: *If any person shall administer or cause to be administered, for
the purpose of affecting the speed of a horse, drugs or stimulants internally,
by hypodermic, or other methods [such person] shall be warned off.*

The best epitaph for the dopers, who ran riot here for half-a-dozen
years, was the remark of a respectable visiting Yankee at Newmarket.
Someone murmured to him that it seemed half the rogues in America
had come to England. He snorted, 'Half? Why, I think you have *all*
of them here!'

At Druid's Lodge, they might have been tempted by dope, but not
for long. At the time when the Americans were carrying all before
them, Fallon came by a bottle of the 'right stuff,' and administered it
to one of the stable's lesser lights. The horse ran nowhere. The jockey
told Fallon he was glad to dismount. 'I've nearly choked with the

smell of that stuff you gave him.' It transpired that Fallon's contact had mistakenly given him a bottle of chloroform.

On another occasion, at Warwick races, Jack was persuaded by a supposed Austrian doctor to part with a tenner for an injection of what he claimed was radium. Nobody ever found out what the dose really was. At all events, after the good doctor had packed his medicine chest and taken his leave, the horse burst the stable door open and ran wild round the streets of Warwick all night. 'After that,' Fallon said, 'I came to the conclusion that good old-fashioned training was sufficient for me.'

4.

Merry Methodist

WITH OR WITHOUT dope, Druid's Lodge was no overnight success. Building was still underway, there was any amount of work to do on the gallops, and Fallon reported that the horses had a touch of the virus. As a result, 1896 went by without a win on the flat. That didn't deter Purefoy from regular purchases at the sales during the year, including – for just £54 – a five-year-old mare, Miss Hoyden, who a few years later bred him an Eclipse winner.

The stable didn't have long to wait to break its duck in 1897. On the third day of the season's opening meeting at Lincoln in March, Frank Forester's Tender and True won a sprint handicap and a modest £185 prize. It wasn't any great event for Forester, whose Cleveland colours of pink and black stripes, black cap with gold tassel, had been seen on the racecourse for five years previously. Nor was it the prelude to any sudden torrent of winners for the Confederates. Two months went by before the next Druid's Lodge success, with Forester's Quadruped in a Bath seller. Nothing could have suggested to the racing world that they'd seen the scouting party of a whole army of future winners, or could have warned the

bookmakers of the remorseless, patient sharpening of knives behind
the stable walls. Tender and True won again at Bath – a handicap
worth the equivalent of £35,570 – and Purefoy got off the mark with
Arcady at Salisbury a few days later. Then after two more minor
winners came an afternoon at Hurst Park that showed, suddenly
and spectacularly, what Fallon could accomplish when the horse and
the price were right. It was the August bank holiday Monday, and
Druid's Lodge sent four horses to Happy Hampton. The first bullet
in the chamber was Holmer Peard's Street Preacher, a two year old
not seen out since a distinctly unpromising debut run at Bath nine
weeks earlier. There, he'd been among the '100–6 others,' and ran
accordingly. At Hurst Park, the betting said everything. After a few
glimpses of 14–1, Street Preacher appeared next at 10–1 and was then
charged down through all rates to 5–2. The gamble was landed in
style: Street Preacher whizzed up Hurst Park's five furlongs and
won with consummate ease by four lengths. The pay-out was hardly
completed when Frank Forester's Jack Snipe was heavily supported
in a selling handicap, and won cheekily by half a length. Like most
of the Confederates' runners in sellers, Jack Snipe was there to be
sold if he won, and he was let go for the minimum bid of £100. Two
races later Forester struck again with Tender and True, a solid 3–1
chance who led at half way and put three lengths between himself
and his pursuers. Then First King completed the four-timer in
another selling handicap.

The racing papers' coverage of Fallon's feat was congratulatory in
a straightforward way. Later successes, particularly in big handicaps,
came to be greeted with heavy sarcasm. But for the moment, here
was a young trainer no one knew, and there was pleasant surprise
at a feat far rarer then than it is now. If the rest of the 1897 season
was an anti-climax, it none the less drew to a close with the highly
satisfactory tally of 15 wins, netting £2,700 prize money.

At the beginning of 1898, with Druid's Lodge completed and fit
to accommodate Percy Cunliffe in his accustomed style, his colours
of white, black seams and cap were registered for the first time. He
wasted no time in entering the fray – his first runner was on the
opening day at Lincoln – but he had to wait until 19 May for his first
winner, Mowbray. He had three other wins during the campaign.
Overall, the season went on as the previous year had ended, with
a satisfactory if unspectacular tally – 10 winners and £1,755. The
highlight was a double for Frank Forester at the big Goodwood
meeting in July. Bourton Hill and the reliable Tender and True won
valuable handicaps on successive days, Tender and True landing a
touch from 100–7 down to 10–1.

With the start of the last year of the nineteenth century, Druid's
Lodge really hit its stride. Cunliffe sent a filly all the way to Liverpool
to win a seller at the season's second meeting, and in the first four
weeks the stable had seven successes. On the opening day of the
Derby meeting at Epsom, Frank Forester landed what *The Sporting
Life* called a 'quite unique double event' in winning the afternoon's two
big handicaps. The first was the Egmont Plate, and Bourton Hill was
a controversial winner. Not seen out for seven weeks, Bourton Hill
had run badly and unbacked in early-season handicaps at Lincoln
and Warwick. He didn't seem a likely runner at Epsom, materialising
at the course and in the paddock at the last possible moment. The
Ring went 5–1 the field to find a favourite among the 14 runners, and
Bourton Hill was immediately the subject of sustained support down
to 11–4 clear favourite. He made every yard of the running.

The stewards enquired whether Forester was 'Satisfied that the
previous running of the horse was consistent with his performance?'
and showed him dismissive press reports of the gelding's previous
runs. Forester had an enquiry of his own: 'Surely the likes of you
aren't going to pay attention to that rubbish?' His response went into

the record as 'satisfactory.' For good measure, Fallon sent out the now six year old Tender and True an hour later to win the Epsom Plate. Tender and True eased from 5–1 out to 100–15, which wasn't at all typical of Druid's Lodge's winning horses that year. In the month after Epsom, the Confederates had ten winners, including a walk-over. The extent to which the stable betted was reflected in the starting prices: 100–30, Evens, Evens, 5–2, 4–1, 4–6, Evens, 4–7 and 8–11.

One of the even-money shots provoked further wrath from the stewards. Fallon had bought a yearling colt for £200 at Ascot sales. Gelded, named Creolin, and registered in Cunliffe's colours, he was one of the outsiders in a poorly-contested early-season auction plate at Gatwick. He made no show. Then at Newmarket's first July meeting, Creolin appeared in a well-subscribed stakes race. There were only seven runners. Five were newcomers. The only other runner with a previous outing had form as moderate as Creolin's. Money didn't so much talk as shriek: Creolin appeared at 5–4 and was returned at Evens. 'Judging by the state of the market, nothing had any chance against Creolin,' remarked *The Sportsman*, and so it proved. He sauntered home by three lengths. Not surprisingly, there were what the *Racing Calendar* described as 'rumours with regard to this race.'

Horses who make no show in auction plates don't as a rule get backed for all the money on the racecourse in £81,270-to-the-winner races on their next outing. They certainly don't win such events in a common canter. Creolin having proved the exception, the Jockey Club hauled in Percy Cunliffe to explain both the horse's previous running and 'the rumour that he had been backed for large sums by his owner and the stable.' By the time Cunliffe saw the stewards, though, it was apparent that despite its valuable prize, Creolin's race had attracted about the worst field imaginable. Two of the seven were so unsound that they never made it to a racecourse again and the others, Creolin included, never won a race between them. The Confederates' horse was simply the best of a very poor bunch, and if not everyone knew whether Creolin was fancied or not, plenty would have known that the others weren't. Once the hoo-ha had subsided, very little went wrong for Druid's Lodge for the remainder of the season. They sent out 13 more winners, including three in a row one Saturday at Alexandra Park.

The 1899 season ended with 29 winners and £7,725 in winnings. Holmer Peard's three-year-old Merry Methodist was the stable star, with six wins and a second from nine outings. His narrow win in Sandown's Foal Stakes contributed far and away the year's biggest prize, £1,974.

Merry Methodist was an almost coppery chestnut with a white star on his forehead. He had a gentle time as a two year old. The only race he was 'off' for was a nursery at Lingfield. The Confederates backed him down to favourite, but were the victims of a muddled start presided over by the ex-jockey Harry Custance. He asked Merry Methodist's lad to walk him back from the tapes, forgot him, and let the rest go with Merry Methodist many lengths in arrears and facing the wrong way. As a consequence, Merry Methodist was never really in a race in his first season. So despite his busy time as a three year old there was reason for Fallon to hope for further improvement – even to start thinking for the first time about a top handicap, and a real cut at the ante-post bookmakers.

Fallon's first thought in 1900 was to aim Merry Methodist at Epsom's City and Suburban handicap in April, but Peard's colt went lame. The touts reported him back in strong work early in May, but the consensus was that he couldn't possibly be got ready for Kempton's Jubilee on 12 May. So little thought was given to Merry Methodist that three days before the Jubilee he stood at 33–1.

They'd reckoned without Fallon's genius for patching up a wrong 'un. Purefoy was poised to make the Ring rattle. Merry Methodist was slashed to 100–6 on the Thursday and 10–1 on Friday. On the day of the race the plunge continued – down to 6–1 to win, 13–8 a place. A rival camp declared for an Australian horse, The Grafter, backed on the course from 10–1 to 7–2.

Paddock critics reckoned Merry Methodist trained to the second: 'No fitter candidate cantered to post.' He was ridden by a seasoned American jockey, Ben Rigby, with a penchant for furious front-running. The 'Special Commissioner' of *The Sporting Life* opined that the pace set by Merry Methodist in the Jubilee 'knocked the great majority of his opponents off their legs in their first quarter mile.'

Coming round the turn, Rigby had Merry Methodist six lengths clear, and the stick handy to keep him there. The top-weights in the race, The Grafter among them, were miles behind, and only Royal Flush (with the benefit of abnormal substances) and the outsider Sirenia were within hailing distance. Halfway up the straight Merry Methodist was still clear, and the flyweight Sirenia – 33–1, and the same price when winning the Duke of York Stakes the autumn before – had passed Royal Flush. In the shadows of the stands, disaster. Flat out, under the whip, Merry Methodist jibbed at a covered path running across the course to the Silver Ring. He made to jump it, hesitated, checked his stride, and lost momentum. Driving for the line, with Rigby flailing away in the saddle, Merry Methodist was headed by Sirenia. The moment he saw company, Merry Methodist put his head down and battled back. A stride past the post, he was in front, but on the line – on the nod – the filly had the call by the shortest of short heads.

There were some long faces in the unsaddling enclosure. As *The Sporting Life* confirmed, Sirenia had upset 'one of the biggest coups of recent times, and saved the Ring many thousands of pounds' – in the region of £30,000, rumour had it. The normally imperturbable Cunliffe was beside himself with rage. Rigby didn't improve matters by acting the cheeky chappie, and Cunliffe was goaded into wishing him a good kicking. The boot was precisely what he got. He made some small amends for Druid's Lodge by winning the afternoon's last race and a few good bets on an un-named filly of Forester's, and then never had another ride for the stable.

Merry Methodist didn't forget Rigby's thrashing that afternoon. Time and again Druid's Lodge set him aside for a big handicap. Time and again, they put down their cash and left it behind. He was backed from 9–2 to 5–2 to win Goodwood's Chesterfield Cup. It was an abysmal race where his 7st 13lb was top weight, yet he contrived to run eighth of nine. He was a similar disappointment in a big handicap at Derby – nineteenth of 21 – and he made no show in the sensational Cambridgeshire which resulted in Tod Sloan's warning off.

Long after his heyday, Sloan has an enduring place in the language. Not just the racing world's description of his style – he was the original 'monkey up a stick' – but the Cockney slang 'On yer Tod' (on yer own: Sloan). Sloan was part of the unprecedented American invasion of English racing at the end of the nineteenth century. He was saint and sinner in equal measure – as great a jockey as Danny Maher, as big a rogue as the Reiffs. Not that he was particularly associated with the dopers. He was simply a punter, and on an heroic scale. They called Tod the monkey up a stick because he was the first to ride short on an English racecourse. Until he burst on the scene, even the champion jockeys had a length of leather associated with the Horse Guards.

Tod Sloan also revolutionised race-riding tactics. We're regularly reminded of the precision of the best American jockeys' perception of how fast a good horse should go. Braulio Baeza on Roberto, Willie Shoemaker on Hawaiian Sound and Steve Cauthen on Slip Anchor have all demonstrated front-running brilliance in major races here. In his generation, Sloan was a sensation. The obvious – that if you're on the best horse, pace throughout the race is the surest way of asserting the fact – didn't seem so obvious till Sloan came along. Its corollary, that an inferior horse can sometimes slip the others in a slowly run race, was just a bonus for Sloan's punters. 'Sloan taught us how races should be run, right through at top speed instead of doddering along for three parts of the journey,' wrote Wilfred Purefoy.

In the autumn of 1900, Sloan and his pals reckoned they'd found a good thing for the Cambridgeshire. At Druid's Lodge, Fallon hadn't entirely given up hope that Merry Methodist might be persuaded to put his best foot forward. He was chasing moonbeams. Tod's selected was a three-year-old French colt called Codoman that he'd ridden to win a £4,000 prize at Longchamp at the beginning of October. Codoman was an easy winner that day, as well he might be. He'd been placed after a rough passage in the Grand Prix de Deauville, was second in the Prix du Jockey Club, and had run up a hat-trick in big races at Maisons-Laffitte between April and July. You couldn't call Codoman a dark horse, yet chauvinism or ignorance led the English handicapper and the bookies to ignore him.

This near classic winner, with around £400,000 in seasonal win and place money, was allocated just 8st in the Cambridgeshire – and any offers in the early betting. He picked up a 10lb penalty for his win at Longchamp, but that didn't weaken Sloan's conviction that Codoman was the ready-made Cambridgeshire winner. Sloan and his pals employed the commission agent Charlie Mills to get their money on. This done, and Codoman still standing at the generous odds of 100–7, Sloan paused for a careful look at the Cambridgeshire weights. The more he looked, there was nothing English-trained – the Jubilee pair Sirenia and Merry Methodist included – to threaten his bets. The only possible danger seemed to him the four-year-old Berrill, trained in Ireland, and set to carry 7st 7lb.

Berrill was, like Codoman, overlooked in the betting, having flopped when well backed a fortnight earlier in the Cesarewitch. His optimum trip was unfathomable. Earlier successes at Cork Park, the Curragh and Cork again had been over 14 furlongs, five furlongs, and then two miles. Tod knew a dark 'un when he saw it, and enquiries were made to establish whether or not Berrill was 'intended' for the Cambridgeshire. He was. In the run-up to the race, Sloan and his punters tried repeatedly to neutralise the threat. A friendly jockey was suggested to Phillie Behan, Berrill's trainer. Behan stuck by his own apprentice, John Thompson – later seven times Irish champion jockey. Attempts were made to buy the rider and nobble the horse. All to no avail: Berrill went to post the trier that Sloan had feared, and the race confirmed his judgement. Berrill made every post a winning one, and won comfortably. Codoman never got in a blow, but was a clear-cut second. Tod flew into an uncontrollable rage in the unsaddling enclosure, cursing Thompson, Behan and the other Berrill connections. The tantrum continued into the weighing room.

The stewards of the Jockey Club, who had this performance enacted before their eyes, were swift to call Tod to account. They knew what he had at stake – it ran into millions in our money – since Sloan had talked openly in Newmarket about his coup. One of his punters was fined a nominal penalty of £25 for offering him 'a large present' in the event of Codoman winning. Charlie Mills was similarly dealt with for working the commission. The stewards' full fury fell on Tod: he was told that he needn't apply for a licence to ride again. Shortly afterwards he sailed from Liverpool to New York.

The epitaph for the jockey who had a greater influence than any other on modern European riding styles was a supporter's parody of Charles Wolfe's lines on *The Burial of Sir John Moore*:

Not a cheer was heard, not a rustling note,
As his traps to the steamer we hurried,
No punter discharged a farewell shot,
O'er the drinks where our sorrows we buried.

We buried them deeply, one, two and three,
The ice in the goblet spurning
With the blinding teardrops falling free
At the thought of his sudden returning.

No useless jacket enclosed his breast,
Nor in sweaters for wasting we bound him,
But we left him – magnanimous – taking his rest,
With his winning mounts around him.

Few and short were the toasts we drank,
Though the Jockey Club wasn't omitted –
The stern J C we had got to thank
For the manner our Toddy had quitted.

Lightly they'll talk of the jockey that's gone,
And perhaps for his seconds upbraid him:
But what does he care? He's the invincible Sloan
In the game that the Briton has played him!

Two thirds of our farewell drinks were done,
When the bell tolled the hour for retiring
So as well as we could, we cheered for Sloan,
His heart with fresh courage inspiring.

By the very next train we came to town,
To the field of his fame undiminished,
And we got ourselves interviewed all up and down,
Till Tod's story of glory was finished.

The 1900 Cambridgeshire didn't have such dire consequences for Druid's Lodge. But a good few bets had again been left in the bookies' satchels by another miserable run from Merry Methodist. He went through the whole of the 1901 season without a win, though favourite as often as not. He flopped again in both the Jubilee – 'Immensely fancied by his party and carries a lot of money,' according to *The Sporting Life* – and the Cambridgeshire, where he made the early running before dropping right out. More frustrating was his second, after some serious betting, in the Peveril of the Peak plate at Derby. 'The failure of Merry Methodist to win after he had looked like coming in alone proves that he is now utterly unreliable,' asserted *Sporting Sketches*: 'Had he run his race out he must have won two or three lengths.'

In 1902, by which time Holmer Peard had become disenchanted with Merry Methodist, and had passed him on to Purefoy, he did at last get his head in front again, including wins on successive days in October. *Sporting Sketches* didn't believe he'd turned over a new leaf:

He will doubtless win races when properly placed where his opponents [can't] go fast enough to get him out of a canter, but he is as likely as ever to turn it up when 'pinched.' The fact is the horse has never forgotten the gruelling he received when beaten by Sirenia for the Jubilee Stakes, and when he hears the whips crack he deems it time to retire from business.

Fortune has a curious way of evening things out. And although she took almost three years to show her hand, she'd presented the

Confederates with the means to avenge Merry Methodist within a few weeks of that first, hugely expensive defeat in the 1900 Jubilee. They were at Hurst Park one afternoon at the end of August to preside over a successful little gamble on a horse of Peard's in a boys' handicap. Everything went nicely to plan. The horse was backed to odds on, and bolted up by six lengths. Equally interesting to the Confederates was the outcome of the two year old seller that day. To the general surprise of most racegoers, one of the entries in this moderate race was a well-bred American import, Ypsilanti, who'd run well when close up fifth of 32 in a Newmarket maiden.

As soon as Ypsilanti's number went into the frame, there was a general rush to back him. He started at 4–6, and won comfortably, as his previous form suggested he should. And for anyone who wondered why this promising colt was running in a seller, the reason was plain to see. He had a large, unsightly swelling on his off-fore pastern. Fallon had a quick look at the leg and – ignoring the paddock asides about 'three good legs and a swinger' – advised Cunliffe to buy him at the auction. The advice wasn't appreciated by Ypsilanti's owner, the redoubtable 'Boss' Croker. Richard Croker was an awkward man to cross. Born in Tipperary, taken to America as a toddler, and put to work at 13 as a fitter in a machine shop, Croker joined the ranks of the notorious New York Democratic institution, Tammany Hall. It was legendary for corruption on a quite staggering scale. A previous 'boss' was arraigned for stealing $6 million (possibly *$400 million* now) from city funds. With impeccable Irish–American connections and a convincing way with his fists, Croker in due course became 'Boss' himself, and prospered mightily. Then along came Theodore Roosevelt with an assault on Tammany, and 'Boss' deemed it prudent to find a new life in the Old World. If his dubious background – which included a murder charge for shooting an opponent during an election campaign – wasn't enough to put up the Turf Establishment's backs, he also proclaimed rabid republican sentiments and the superiority of American bloodstock.

The story was that he came by his first string when a San Francisco hotel-keeper decided to withdraw from racing. The man had a number of racehorses, and also a harem of pretty girls who used to entertain the punters in his saloons. He encouraged trade by parading the girls in the club enclosures at local race meetings. The stewards were outraged. They called the hotelier in, accused him of 'moral turpitude,' and issued an ultimatum. 'The whores go, or the horses go.' The man stayed loyal to his human fillies, and Croker bought the equine ones. One result was a handsome bay colt by Galore (a son of the 1875 Derby winner Galopin), out of Stefanette (USA), called Ypsilanti after the town near Detroit where he was foaled.

Croker's trainer Wishard did his best to keep Ypsilanti after the Hurst Park seller, first by drawing loud attention to the lump on his leg, then by bidding up to 400 guineas. But a final nod from Percy Cunliffe won the day at 420 guineas. When Fallon got Ypsilanti back to Druid's Lodge it didn't take him long to discover, as he'd hoped, that the colt was 'A long, long way above plating class. The form he showed on our gallops told me he wouldn't have been dear at 10 times the price.'

Wishard probably imagined he could get Ypsilanti back the first time he ran for Cunliffe in a seller. But Fallon had much better things in mind for Ypsilanti, beginning with a £500 nursery at Derby in November. Danny Maher was booked to ride. The incomparable Maher – as acceptable a face of American racing as Sloan, Reiff and the dopers were unacceptable – was in his first season in England. He had to put up 3 lb overweight to ride Ypsilanti at 7st 13lb, but the Confederates weren't deterred from a punt. In a field of twenty-five, Ypsilanti was backed from 8–1 to 5–1 clear favourite. He ran a big race – never out of the first three – but came up against a flyweight who later turned out useful, and had to settle for second.

Cunliffe and the others were in no way disappointed. They'd seen enough to know there'd be other days for Ypsilanti, and as the curtain came down on the 1900 season they could look back on 26 winners and £5,232 in win and place money. Once again, all the Confederates had been in the winner's enclosure, Edward Wigan having a tremendous year with 14 successes. The near-miss with Peard's Merry Methodist in the Jubilee was followed by a good third for Wigan's The Reeve when sharing favouritism for the Hunt Cup, but overall the stable policy remained as before – a high strike rate in minor races.

The 1901 season began with a lucrative double from Ypsilanti. At Liverpool on the fourth day of the flat, he was backed from 3–1 to 2–1 to beat six rivals, and made all for a comfortable win under Danny Maher. Then Fallon ran Ypsilanti over 10 furlongs in Kempton's £1,000 May Plate. He was friendless in the market behind a colt called Pietermaritzburg that all concerned reckoned a certainty. Hardly surprisingly, since Pietermaritzburg went on to run fourth in the St Leger and then won the Jockey Club Stakes and £725,000 at Newmarket – form that would normally take care of the winner of a seller. Ypsilanti was held up in the early stages, got a tremendous run up the rails in the straight and wore down Pietermaritzburg in the last 50 yards to win by three-quarters of a length. That was his winning done for the season, though three times he ran well to be placed in valuable handicaps.

5.

The Jubilee Jackpot

FALLON SHOWED REMARKABLE consistency in the 1901 season, sending out 26 winners of £5,105 in win and place earnings. Percy Cunliffe had the winners of eight races, Edward Wigan seven. Pure had the satisfaction of nine wins, six of them from his colt Templemore. Equally satisfying, when Templemore won on successive days at Worcester in October he was providing a young Druid's Lodge apprentice with his first-ever wins. The apprentice was Bernard Dillon. Bernard – Ben to the racing fraternity – came from Tralee. He was recommended to Pure by a hunting friend in Tipperary. The notion of a stable jockey was beginning to appeal to the Confederates, but they had a phobia about letting any of the established jockeys near the stable or the gallops. They knew very well that many of them betted extravagantly, including champions like Otto Madden whose nephew was a lad at Druid's Lodge. On the other hand, it was a disadvantage not being able to count on a top rider's availability when required. Danny Maher was already in demand from stables with classic horses. And sometimes the hired gun fired a blank, as Rigby had on Merry Methodist.

Ben Dillon was only 14 when he came to Druid's Lodge. His elder brother Joe was already apprenticed to Purefoy. Ben was a brilliant jockey in the making – calm, confident, nerveless when the money was down, as of course it often was. He was welcomed, too, by the other lads. He had a pleasant voice to sing an Irish ballad, and he played the accordion to wile away the dull nights on Salisbury Plain. His style of riding can be inferred from his nickname 'Butcher Ben', but whip-happiness isn't something that a gambling stable minds much. As good a jockey as he turned out to be – in a sadly short career he was to ride 455 winners, at a strike rate of 18 per cent – he was lucky to arrive at Druid's Lodge when he did.

Fallon's capabilities had been underlined by successive seasonal tallies of 29, 26 and 26 wins – over 100 in five years. From their own studs, from the sales and from selling-race auctions, the Confederates sent him a bumper crop of horses to train for 1902. The result was a bumper crop of winners. Fallon sent out the winners of 44 races and £14,872. The major beneficiaries were Purefoy with 18 winners and Ben Dillon with 16. Forester, Cunliffe and Wigan had nine, eight and seven successes respectively. Only Holmer Peard, with just two winners, seemed to miss out, but his responsibilities at Cork Park and the new course at Phoenix Park kept him in Ireland. Several of his horses were passed on to Purefoy.

Ben Dillon's brother Joe rode nine winners, the rest being shared out among outsiders who had most of the mounts on the stable high-weights. All in all, though, 1902 was a communal triumph for Druid's Lodge. In recent times a Newmarket trainer was reported as saying, after a year when a fair few stable fancies had obliged, that his lads 'came to work on bicycles in the spring and in cars by the autumn.' Had the lads at Druid's Lodge not all been living in captivity, something similar would have been seen there at the end of 1902. As Fallon remarked, 'One way and another we backed 'em all.'

To put the yard's year into perspective, its 44 winners equate to over 130 nowadays, simply on the basis of the greater number of races held. Making allowance for the out-of-reach racecourses of the north and Scotland, Fallon's achievements in 1902 become value for perhaps 150 wins nowadays.

One training feat of Fallon's that year needs no adjustments or allowances. In a five-day blitz at the end of October, he sent 19 runners to four meetings – and came back with 14 winners and three placings. On the Monday, one of the stable's two runners at Wolverhampton was hot favourite for the nursery handicap, made all and won in a canter. The following day at Gatwick, Purefoy's Templemore – second in the Jockey Club Stakes three weeks earlier – was backed, not surprisingly, from 4–6 to 2–5 before an easy win in the Gatwick Stakes. The next race saw another easy Druid's Lodge win in the seller.

On the second day at Gatwick the stable had three runners. All won. Merry Methodist was backed from 6–4 to 4–6 and beat three rivals in a canter. Another successful gamble (5–2 from 4–1) followed on Purefoy's Orphrey, and Frank Forester's Lady Drake completed the hat-trick in a nursery. The minimum winning distance of the trio was four lengths.

The next day at Sandown saw Merry Methodist make all, and land another gamble from 9–4 to 7–4. Templemore then handed out a 10-length thrashing to the Cesarewitch (and subsequent Jockey Club Cup) winner Black Sand. The same afternoon at Worcester, Druid's Lodge was landing a short-priced treble. Two of the wins were in sellers, and the stable let both go in the auctions. It's a mystery that anyone bothered bidding for Druid's Lodge horses after these bad races. Fallon had usually worked wonders to get some duck-hearted or unsound animal to the starting gate, let alone to win with it. The frequent outcome was that the new connections failed abjectly. The two sold at Worcester – both to the minimum bid – confirmed the pattern. One never ran again, the other never won.

The Friday produced two more winners at Worcester. Of greater significance for the future, a chestnut gelding of Forester's called Uninsured won the two year old maiden at Sandown. The 'Man in the Ring' reported that Uninsured was always an even money chance, and 'carried at that rate an enormous amount of money.' All of it returned whence it came, with interest. Uninsured shot clear at halfway, and won pulling up by six lengths. By any standards, the week was a remarkable feat of stable management by Fallon. With the limited transport facilities then available, it stands comparison with Michael Dickinson's celebrated 12 winners from 21 runners at six courses on Boxing Day 1982.

The Confederates' final winner of 1902 – Purefoy's Amphlett in mid-November – typified their season, coming in a small handicap at a minor track and at odds on. The big races continued to elude them. Their biggest pay-day wasn't even a winner. Pure's Templemore collected a handsome place stake – *£151,200* – in finishing second at Newmarket to the Derby, Eclipse and St Leger runner-up Rising Glass, with the Derby winner Ard Patrick back in third. Small wonder that Jack Fallon named his second son John Templemore Fallon.

Another notable win was recorded by Ypsilanti in the Chesterfield Cup at Goodwood. It wasn't a strongly contested race, but it was enough for Fallon to tell Cunliffe that it was just a matter of time before one of the big handicaps came Ypsilanti's way. Cunliffe's selected was the Lincoln at the start of the 1903 season. It was a unique Lincoln, in having the weights headed by the winner of four classics – Sceptre. She, one of the best English race mares of all time, was running to get Bob Sievier out of a hole. 'It was money, as always, or rather lack of it, that compelled him to run Sceptre,' wrote John

Welcome in his biography of Sievier, *Neck or Nothing*. 'He knew the distance was too short for her and the time of year too early. It would have been kinder and wiser to have cut his losses and sold her, but this the gambler in him would not let him do.'

Sceptre had 9st 11b. Ypsilanti had 7st 9lb, had wintered well, and the Confederates speculated each way and at long odds. Sceptre, despite 'her owner's freely expressed misgivings,' was second favourite for the race: Ypsilanti went off at 20–1. Sceptre was brisk and eager in the parade. Ypsilanti attracted comment for his fitness and well-being, and was always in the leading group. Sceptre had every chance below the distance but close home the weight told. She was eased to finish fifth. Ypsilanti, reported *The Sporting Life*, 'Did what his clever party expected – gained a place,' and though he only held on narrowly to third behind two outsiders, the place odds were better business than the cramped win price of most of the Druid's Lodge fancies around that time.

There had, too, been an interesting piece of advice for Fallon to ponder. It came from Charlie 'Old England' Hannan, the biggest professional punter for a period spanning almost 50 years. Hannan hadn't backed Ypsilanti, but he concluded that the colt would just about have won had he been able to take a 'breather.' 'That horse of yours will never win a race on a straight course. You'll have to run him round a turn,' he told Fallon. Everything fell into place. Six weeks ahead was a handicap with a big prize, run round a bend, and over a course where Ypsilanti was already a winner. It was, for good measure, a race with a strong ante-post betting market: Kempton's Great Jubilee handicap. 'Ypsilanti wasn't exactly flung in with 8st 11b,' recalled Fallon, but 'I now had him so well that I felt more than confident. Druid's Lodge began backing the horse the moment a market was formed.' The stable commission was launched at 25–1, and snowballed to the extent that on the Monday before the race

Ypsilanti was down to 8–1. There the odds stayed till the Saturday. In the parade, the deep-shouldered Ypsilanti again drew praise for his condition. Up above, lightning crackled in a pitch-black sky, and a thunderstorm raged all round Sunbury. The ground was a swamp – the final inducement for the racing public to take Ypsilanti's leg on trust. He was backed down to 7–2 clear favourite.

The race was sweet recompense for Merry Methodist. After taking a lead for the first couple of furlongs, Ben Dillon rushed Ypsilanti to the front, took a pull at the turn into the straight, and won by a length and a half without turning a hair. 'Coming into the straight the favourite was doing little more than cantering,' reported the *Irish Field*: '[He] scored one of the easiest handicap victories ever seen.'

The result was greeted with a great deal of public enthusiasm, since most racegoers had joined in the gamble. It was assumed that 'Boss' Croker would be a good man to avoid. He'd not only let the Jubilee winner go for 420 guineas; the Chester Cup had been won three days before by an animal called Vendale that 'Boss' had lost for £100 after another seller. Some double! The blow was cushioned, though, by Fallon. Once the Confederates' commission had been worked, he let Croker's trainer Enoch Wishard know that Ypsilanti was 'expected,' so the Americans too had their cut.

No such consolation was available to the connections of the Jubilee runner-up, Duke of Westminster. He collected just £200 for his efforts – less than one per cent of the staggering £22,000 that George Faber, the MP for York, had paid for the colt the previous year. Faber was brilliantly duped by Bob Sievier, who in the usual pressing circumstances had two horses for sale. One was Duke of Westminster, who he thought useless. The other was his adored Sceptre. Sievier deceived Faber's trainer by asking vastly more for the colt than for Sceptre, creating the impression that something must be amiss with the filly. How these things turn out: Duke of

Westminster had cost Sievier 5,600 guineas on the same afternoon that he bought Sceptre. The colt was then sold to the unfortunate Faber for £22,000 and he struggled, eventually, to win a three-horse race at Ascot. Ypsilanti was bought out of a seller and beat 'The Duke' in the Jubilee, giving him weight.

For Cunliffe and the Confederates, Ypsilanti's win was the culmination of seven years' investment and planning. They hit the jackpot. Fallon alone had £8,000 to come from the Ring. By his reckoning, his masters probably scooped, in our money, well over £7 *million*. And it was only the beginning; the bookmakers who cringed after Ypsilanti's Jubilee had something far nastier in store for them: Hackler's Pride.

6.

Hackler's Pride

'AT THE FINISH it was only a question as to how many lengths little Jarvis intended Hackler's Pride to win by. The judge gave it as three. It might have been 33.' That was the verdict of *Sporting Luck* on the result of the 1903 Cambridgeshire. Hackler's Pride's win was one of the greatest betting coups ever landed on the British turf, and possibly *the* greatest.

The Druid's Lodge filly was bred by P. Quinlan in 1900 in County Limerick, by Hackler out of Comma. Hackler, by the 1876 2,000 Guineas and St Leger winner Petrarch, was the winner of four races, a racehorse of merit without being top class. He let down into a fine stallion and headed the Irish list of winning sires in 1900 and 1901. His fee was a modest thirty guineas. Comma was useless on the racecourse. She failed in such lowly company as the Eglington Hunt members' race. She had, though, already thrown minor winners.

Hackler's Pride realised 75 guineas as a yearling at the Ballsbridge August sales. She was a big bay with a rather common head. One judge thought her mean-looking and Fallon later called her an ugly duckling. She was bought by Willie Rankin, Ireland's biggest professional punter.

She made her racecourse debut at the Curragh's April meeting in 1902 in a five-furlong juvenile plate. Rankin clearly wasn't entertaining an angel unawares. Hackler's Pride was backed from 10–1 down to 4–1 second favourite to beat 21 rivals, only one of whom, Roe O'Neill, was a previous winner. He started favourite. In receipt of 5lb, Hackler's Pride finished two lengths in front of him, but was herself beaten a length by Gold Lock, the 'declared to win' of Major Eustace Loder's three runners in the race. Gold Lock had the advantage of the rails all the way. Out in the centre of the course, Hackler's Pride was always prominent, and ran on strongly in the last furlong.

After her promising debut, Hackler's Pride was put by for the autumn, not appearing till the end of August at the Phoenix Park. She was raised in class, running in a £1,000 five-furlong plate. Despite reports that she hadn't been working well, she was prominent in the betting, and again ran a race full of promise. Conceding 4lb to the Bernard Dillon-partnered Bushey Belle, she was beaten only three quarters of a length, and reckoned unlucky at that.

Crucially for Hackler's Pride's future, the unplaced hot favourite for the race was an un-named filly of Frank Forester's. In the stands in his capacity as the Phoenix Park's manager, Holmer Peard watched the race with more than usual interest. Time would show that he rated it the best possible maiden form. The winner, Bushey Belle, was bought for £1,500 by Percy Cunliffe; she later bred him an Oaks winner. The second, Hackler's Pride, would go to Frank Forester. The fourth, Lord Rossmore, was sold to Cunliffe later in the year, and won him the 1903 Irish Derby. As for Forester's un-named filly, she came to be called Lady Drake and more than paid her way.

Hackler's Pride's next race also came under Peard's eye. She ran a week later in a handicap at Cork Park. Among Peard's successes at Cork had been substantially increased prize money. At £490 to the winner, the nursery that day offered a large reward for a country meeting. Hackler's Pride didn't collect any of the prize money. She started co-favourite with the eventual winner, but finished only fifth of the eight runners.

Rankin was short of funds, so Peard's subsequent offer to buy Hackler's Pride was timely. Peard had marked Hackler's Pride down as a filly with all the scope in the world. There'd been no disgrace in her fifth place. She carried top weight, finished on the heels of the first four, and came out the best horse in the race at the weights. Peard looked her over and passed her sound. So for £1,500 Hackler's Pride moved from Rankin's hands into the ownership of Frank Forester, and was transferred to Druid's Lodge. It must have seemed a fair return for Rankin. Including the second-place purses, Hackler's Pride brought him £1,720 for his £75 outlay at Ballsbridge. But his profit paled in comparison with the dividends that the Pride was to earn for the Confederacy.

The first weren't long in coming. Joe Dillon rode Hackler's Pride in all her work at Druid's Lodge. Soon, Fallon was confirming Peard's judgement. The Irish filly 'was definitely a smasher. She cleaned out all our two year olds as though they were nothing but donkeys.' She'd also been paid two compliments by her Phoenix Park conqueror; Bushey Belle had twice won easily at the Curragh.

In mid-November, Hackler's Pride was allocated 7st 10lb in the £1,000 Chesterfield Nursery at Derby. The Derby course is long gone, but its valuable end-of-season five-furlong nursery was one of the premier two year old betting races of the year. On the eve of the race, Fallon collected the lads' bets for Hackler's Pride. They amounted to £180. Purefoy was astonished: 'Good Heavens, I thought they'd want about two shillings apiece.' With Ben Dillon's claim, Hackler's Pride carried only 7st 5lb at Derby. She also carried the lads' bets and several thousands invested by the Confederates on Fallon's assurance that she was the goods. The stable confidence ensured that she started favourite. Some visiting Irish punters got 100–8 and 10–1 in the outer enclosures. She was then backed in a rush down to 9–2 to beat 26 other runners. Showing lightning speed from the gate, Hackler's Pride was up with the pace to half-way. Below the distance, she pulled clear to land the gamble by four lengths. The form looked good: seven of the next eight home were previous winners. The exception, the maiden Brambilla, was to win the City and Suburban handicap at Epsom the following spring.

The Confederates weren't to know that, but as winter gathered on Salisbury Plain and Fallon set about building up Hackler's Pride and getting her more fully acclimatised, all manner of enticing options were open to them. The first, perhaps most obvious, was sprinting. The filly had never run over more than five furlongs, and had shown speed enough to be a wide-margin winner at Derby. Big handicaps like the Wokingham at Ascot and the Stewards' Cup at Goodwood offered, then as now, the ante-post betting market that was the Confederates' target. In the event, Hackler's Pride ran in both those big sprints, but without the slightest intention of troubling the judge.

Her first outing as a three year old was over five furlongs, on an April afternoon at Sandown when Purefoy won the Esher Cup with Cappa White. Unfit and unfancied, she finished seventh of 16 runners after showing early speed.

At the beginning of June, Hackler's Pride put up the performance that decided her future, when running the useful Wild Oats to three lengths at Hurst Park, conceding 4lb. The race was over a mile. Still not fit – *The Sporting Life* said she'd 'see a better day' – she was well away. Steadied, she was way off the pace at the turn into the straight, and then ran on with great purpose to be second. After the race Cunliffe decided on the Cambridgeshire as her objective.

As the season progressed, Wild Oats appeared seemingly every other week, running openly and honestly – placed in eight consecutive races, winning three – and providing a series of lines of form to other likely Cambridgeshire candidates. Meanwhile, Hackler's Pride was run neither openly nor honestly. She put in a token appearance in the Wokingham. In pouring rain, she finished in the ruck with Dumbarton Castle, who represented another formidable gambling stable – Percy Bewicke's Grateley – and Bewicke's accomplice from the Stratton SP coup, G. A. Prentice.

Dumbarton Castle was, like Hackler's Pride, a rod in pickle. Hackler's Pride was among the '16–1 the field' favourites in the early betting on the Stewards' Cup. As the Druid's Lodge commission failed to materialise, she drifted out to 25–1 on the day of the race. The Stewards' Cup showed the public, the bookmakers and the handicapper nothing of her ability. It did, though, show Purefoy's far-sightedness and attention to detail.

Ben Dillon, who the previous year had ridden at as low as 6st 7lb, was putting on weight. He found it impossible now to ride below 7st 2lb. But if the Cambridgeshire attracted any top-notchers at the head of the handicap – and if the intended moderate mid-season performances of Hackler's Pride had the desired effect on the handicapper's assessment – then she might get into the race with a flyweight. The Cambridgeshire is no place to carry overweight when the money's down, and Purefoy, four months in advance, set about finding a lightweight jockey to replace Dillon if the occasion required one. His eye fell on Jack Jarvis. He was the 15-year-old son of the Newmarket trainer William Jarvis, and fast becoming the season's star apprentice. He was duly engaged for the Stewards' Cup to get to know Hackler's Pride.

The race was, for all but the Grateley and Druid's Lodge connections, a miserable and unsatisfactory affair, run in torrential rain and thick mist. Jarvis, with no idea of what was planned for October, found Hackler's Pride quiet and amenable on the way to post. Meanwhile, in the Ring an infectious gamble on Dumbarton Castle was gathering pace. The Grateley hope – 33–1 a week previously – had been touted in the London clubs at the weekend as the Stewards' Cup 'business'. Still 20–1 on the morning of the race, Dumbarton Castle was drawn against the inside rail, traditionally an advantage when Goodwood rides soft or heavy. When the draw became known, the money flooded on. At the off Dumbarton Castle was down to 4–1, with no better than 3–1 available to big bets. To compound the misery of the crowd – barely a third of which could get under the stands to shelter from the downpour – the start was held up for 45 minutes. The hiatus was the result of the deliberate delaying tactics of a clique of older jockeys who tried all season to disrupt the newly introduced starting gate.

When finally the field came into view Dumbarton Castle was poised on the heels of the leaders. He cut them down close home, and then slipped and unshipped his rider Otto Madden after the post, but the jockey managed to keep hold of the reins and weighed in safely. The gamble – reportedly £60,000 (over *£5.6 million*) – was safely landed. Oddly, it turned out to be the last big winner for the Grateley syndicate. From that moment on, nothing they fancied and backed achieved anything, and they went their separate ways within months. Behind Dumbarton Castle, Hackler's Pride finished demurely in mid-field. None of the race-readers recorded any comment on her. 'So many horses were eased quite a good distance from home that little heed should be given to the positions of many of them,' warned one observer.

William Jarvis saw Hackler's Pride's lad having problems getting her rugged up in the wind and rain after the race. He lent a helping hand, and was surprised to be told in a broad Irish brogue to 'Let your little boy ride this one again. She hasn't done a canter for a month.' 'The following week,' Jack Jarvis recalled, 'My father was asked to let the Druid's Lodge stable have a second claim on my services for the rest of the season. We found out afterwards that this was done solely to secure me for the Cambridgeshire.' He didn't see the mare again until Newmarket, nor did he visit Druid's Lodge to ride work on her. One outing was thought sufficient acquaintance by Purefoy. So a back-up jockey had been arranged, with the bonus of his 5lb claim. A couple of quiet runs had been trailed in front of the handicapper. Now the business of seriously training the Pride began.

As in all things connected with the stable, little was left to chance. Until J. V. Rank bought some adjacent fields and extended the gallops in the 1930s, the longest straight piece of work at Druid's Lodge was a mile. So Fallon found a strip of perfect ground at Larkhill Camp, resembling Newmarket right down to a final uphill climb. A nine-furlong gallop was measured and marked. Hackler's Pride and her galloping companions were regularly walked the hour or so to Larkhill for their trials. The tackle was the best that Druid's Lodge could provide: Ypsilanti; the Irish Derby winner Lord Rossmore; Uninsured – winner of four races as a two-year-old; and Frank Forester's smart Lady Drake, the winner of three races in mid-summer. Hackler's Pride's progress was meticulously recorded in Fallon's gallop books. In the newspaper touts' fanciful reports, she was noted over every distance from five to ten furlongs – in company with seemingly every horse on Salisbury Plain.

Early in September, the Cambridgeshire weights were published. Hackler's Pride was allotted just 7st 1lb. Her galloping companions – Ypsilanti, Lady Drake, Lord Rossmore and Uninsured – received 8st 8lb, 7st 7lb, 7st 3lb and 7st respectively. Fallon told Purefoy that Hackler's Pride had at least 10lb in hand. 'Not enough,' replied Pure: 'train her to give us another seven.'

Even a casual look at the handicapper's work, with the substantial benefit of hindsight, shows how Hackler's Pride's only performance of any merit in 1903 had been overlooked. In April she showed herself about the equal of Wild Oats at Hurst Park. At the end of June, Wild Oats gave Lord Howard de Walden's Kilglass a 20lb thrashing at Newmarket. Yet Kilglass, who held a prominent place throughout the ante-post betting on the Cambridgeshire, was set to receive only 7lb from Hackler's Pride.

Again using Wild Oats as a yardstick, Hackler's Pride could be assessed as some 21lb the superior of the admirably consistent Burses, owned by that redoubtable punter Jack Hammond, who started as a stable lad in Captain Machell's yard and was to leave half a million when he died. Burses was being trained for the Cesarewitch-Cambridgeshire double. He had little chance in the Cambridgeshire, in receipt of just 3lb from Hackler's Pride. It's impossible to avoid the conclusion that her 'easy' outings at Ascot and Goodwood had done the trick. The handicapper was well and truly hoodwinked.

To be fair, the twin pillars of handicapping – race reading, and the form book – were different, lesser aids in those days. Now, punters can buy daily papers and weekly form books that give 'close-up' comments on every horse in every race. Distances between horses are given from first place to last. The same data is available with a click or two on the internet. At the beginning of the last century, it was rare for distances or placings to be given beyond the first three. As for race reading, today's punters are in danger of forgetting the days before racecourse commentaries, terrestrial television, At The Races, Racing UK and video recording. Nowadays, dedicated punters can replay a race as many times as there are runners to study. Then, the only way to read a race was to go racing. And as Fallon well knew, a big sprint handicap is as good a place as any to bury a non-trier. Even the best race-reader would be hard pressed to spot every 'easy' in the pell-mell of a multi-runner sprint.

So the Confederates had their horse wonderfully handicapped. The final element in their pre-race preparations was the domain of Purefoy: betting. Every contemporary recollection of Purefoy concurs. He was one of the smartest men at working a big gamble that ever lived. He used the most discreet of the professional commission agents. He and the other Confederates had travelled extensively, so contacts were in place to get money on in Europe, South Africa, Australia and anywhere else with a betting market on the big English races.

Purefoy also had his specials: a network of connections with no known links to Druid's Lodge or, professionally, with racing. One such was a well-known surgeon, Allen Baker; another was a dentist in Woking; a third – among the cleverest of a clever set-up – was a Birmingham station-master, introduced involuntarily by Fallon. He was at New Street station one day to arrange transport to Wolverhampton for a couple of his runners. He was invited into the station-master's office for a drink. The man was a Scot, William Murray. He asked if Fallon had a winner or two by which he might supplement his earnings? 'You know, Mr Fallon,' confided Murray: 'These sort of jobs don't bring you in much money. I've been 30 years in the employ of the railway company, and as far as I can see I'll die a poor man.' Apparently, he'd tried to augment his income by catching thieves. The company rewarded him with just 10 shillings per thief. The hazard-to-reward ratio seemed ungenerous, and Fallon appealed as a better prospect for profit.

Fallon and Murray got to know each other well. When Jack wanted to do some betting on his own account, away from the steely vigilance of Cunliffe and Purefoy, up went his instructions to New Street. Murray opened accounts with a score of the leading bookmakers in the Midlands. Fallon had an account at Lloyds Bank in Birmingham to receive the anticipated dividends. A series of successful commissions was handled by Murray – a dab hand at getting a hundred or two on a horse without the money going back to the course, swore Jack. In turn, Murray, like Purefoy, believed that you could back a horse to win almost any sum, provided you employed the right people for the job. One such was a local parish priest. The Birmingham bookies probably thought they'd found a rare old mug when the reverend cycled round backing Hackler's Pride.

The first speculative prices on the Cambridgeshire began to appear after the publication of the weights at the beginning of September. At the end of September and in early October, Uninsured – at 40–1 and 33–1 – was the only Druid's Lodge horse in the betting. The early fancy prices about Hackler's Pride weren't available for long, or to many, prompting Purefoy to ask Fallon if he knew who'd been backing the filly? 'Me, for one,' was the gist of Fallon's unwise reply. Purefoy was furious. He threatened to scratch Hackler's Pride's engagement. 'Do that, and I'll scratch you from *all* engagements,' retorted Fallon. After an almighty row, mutual self-interest prevailed. Hackler's Pride remained in the Cambridgeshire.

Not until mid-October did she start entering the club call-overs at 25–1, and right up to the eve of the race the Confederates played a pea-and-thimble game with the bookmakers and betting public, with each of their entries ostensibly attracting support. Purefoy had backed Hackler's Pride to win a fortune before the world beyond Salisbury Plain woke up to her being the Druid's Lodge 'pea.' On 5 October, *Sporting Luck* reported her backed 'for something like £10,000' adding that she seemed to have a bit to find, but that 'If her connections consider her capable of doing so, their judgement must be respected. They seldom make blunders.'

When the money was on overseas and through the private connections, the Druid's Lodge commission agents stepped in at the Victoria and Beaufort Club call-overs and on the racecourse.

Some heavy metal began to appear: £2,000 to £80 at the call-over and £3,000 to £180 at Sandown on 24 October, for example. £1,000 to £60 was laid again in the offices two days later; then £1,600 to £100, £1,000 to £60, £3,000 to £200 and £1,000 to £100 on the 27th, followed by £1,500 to £150 and £1,000 to £80 several times on the 28th, two days before the race. These reported bets amounted to over £125,000 in our terms, to win almost £1.8 million. 'It looks now as though the mystery has been solved,' reported The Sporting Life, noting 'numerous other sums' for the Pride.

Percy Cunliffe was adding his own finishing touch. Fallon's pre-emption of the stable commission still rankled. Until shortly before the race there'd been a minority view among the Confederates that Hackler's Pride should be scratched to teach Fallon a lesson. The businessman in Cunliffe didn't believe in cutting off his nose to spite his face. So he sent for a top commission agent, Albert Hamblin, at that time unidentified with Druid's Lodge bets. Cunliffe asked him what outlay would be needed to win £50,000 or so? A sum was mentioned which seemed reasonable. 'Get to work' was the order. On the Tuesday night at Newmarket, an enormous single bet of £11,000 to £1,000 (£97,300 to win £1.07 million) on Hackler's Pride was recorded at the Subscription Rooms.

Hackler's Pride had been working, if possible, better than ever. Racecourse rumour said her final gallop at Larkhill was a stone in front of Forester's Lady Drake. In the race, Lady Drake was set to give 6lb to Hackler's Pride. If she really was now a stone in front of Lady Drake at home, then Fallon had done even better than Purefoy demanded. He'd got her into the Cambridgeshire with around 20lb in hand of the handicapper's assessment. But an unexpected problem intruded: Jack couldn't find a train.

The Confederates had kept their cards against their chests to the last. They sent three Cambridgeshire entries up to London: Hackler's

Pride, Lord Rossmore and Uninsured. There on the Tuesday, Fallon sought a connection to Newmarket. 'No train,' he was told: 'there's only one going today, and that's a special carrying the King.' Fallon thought the King wouldn't mind if a horsebox was attached to the back of his train. 'I'll ask him, if you like,' he added helpfully. The suggestion wasn't well received. But a £5 note changed hands, together with an idea for its profitable investment. The upshot? A second 'special' travelled to Newmarket half an hour behind his Majesty, reserved for Fallon and the Druid's Lodge horses.

The night before the race the rain fell in sheets, backed by a gale. Tucked up warm in Newmarket, those with long memories and a fancy for a coincidence bet might have recalled a similar night 21 years before. Then, the storm continued unabated into Cambridgeshire day. A carriage was blown over on the way to the races, the numbers board tipped over, the meeting was postponed for a day, and the race was won by Hackness – the grand-dam of Hackler's Pride.

On the morning of 30 October the wind had subsided by six o'clock, but few touts faced the elements on the Heath. Those who did saw a new Hackler's Pride; a ball of muscle, pulling double, and showing a tremendous ground-devouring action on the sodden turf. 'She gave a very favourable impression, a beautiful mare with long, level stride. She made many adherents.' Or as *Sporting Luck* put it: 'The murder was out.' On her toes when saddled and later in the paddock, she again caught the eye. Backed down from 8–1 in the morning, she vied for favouritism at 6–1 until a final rush for the hard-trained Kilglass sent him off at 9–2 favourite. The Lincoln winner Over Norton and Burses – third a fortnight earlier in the Cesarewitch – were each 100–12.

Jack Jarvis, who as part of the Druid's Lodge camouflage had been appearing in the papers as Lord Rossmore's jockey, was legged into the saddle with little ceremony. 'When I walked out to the parade ring I was still unaware that Hackler's Pride was a racing certainty. The first thing that happened was that my whip was taken away from me.' 'You won't need that, sonny,' said Fallon. He added that all Hackler's Pride needed was to jump off and run her own race. Finally, Jarvis was told, the protective ankle boots she wore were to guard against hitting herself through her hind action. They would be taken off at the post. A lad had been sent to the start for this purpose. On the way down, disaster almost struck. Jarvis found the supremely fit Hackler's Pride a different proposition to his sedate mount in the Stewards' Cup.

> When I was let go to canter down to the post, away she went and I simply could not hold one side of her. For a few dreadful moments we looked like galloping to Cambridge, taking the stable money with us. Luckily the planning came to the rescue. The lad that had been sent down to the post had just reached the seven furlong starting gate when he saw his filly approaching, obviously out of control. With considerable presence of mind he ran out on to the course and shouted at her. She recognised his voice and eased up just sufficiently for me to get a pull at her. I pulled her round in a circle and as she came by the lad again he grabbed her and led her the rest of the way.

For those days, it was a prompt start, nine minutes from the white flag to the off. Thereafter, in Jarvis's words, 'I was one of the first away, and after a hundred yards I never saw another horse in the race.' *Sporting Luck* asked simply next day: 'What can be written about a two horse race?'

Hackler's Pride and Burses broke quickly and had to all intents and purposes settled their field by half-way. Four lengths back came Le

Souvenir and Kilglass, with a further gap to the rest who presented a
'tremendously long tail.'

> The filly seemed to revel in the mud and the further she
> went, the better she seemed to like it. I must say I never
> saw such a hollow exhibition made of a field in a handicap
> as Hackler's Pride made of the candidates opposed to her.
> It seemed either as if she were a steam engine or that they
> were unable to raise a gallop. Almost from fall of flag it was
> a one-horse race.

At the Bushes, Hackler's Pride led Burses by half a length. As she
met the rising ground, she drew clear, ridden hands and heels to a
comfortable three-length win.

Fallon was in a minority of one in claiming that 'All Newmarket
was shouting itself hoarse with delight.' The phrase 'not a popular
victory' echoed in various forms in the following day's and week's
papers. Some drew attention to the winner's moderate seasonal
form. Others railed against the smokescreen thrown up by Purefoy's
elaborate working of the stable commission. *Sporting Luck* asserted:

> There are few Cambridgeshires I can call to mind which
> provoked so little enthusiasm, and the victory of any other
> runner than Hackler's Pride would have been received with
> much more satisfaction by the general public. The reason
> is not far to seek. The stable had four horses engaged, one
> of which, Ypsilanti, was never thought of by the public.
> But the oracle was worked with the other three to the last
> moment, when many backers who had been taken in over
> Lord Rossmore and Uninsured were so disgusted that they
> let the real 'Simon Pure' run loose. The manner in which

the changes were rung on the two that were never intended
was remarkably clever, but what the stable had up their sleeve
it is just possible that even they themselves did not know
the full strength of it. It may be summed up in four words.
It was no race.

Truth reported that

Hackler's Pride won her race with consummate ease, but
her victory certainly was not a popular one, as it is utterly
impossible to reconcile this form with her defeats at Ascot,
Goodwood, and other meetings. She must have either been
unfit or out of form during the summer, and all things
considered, most people were of the opinion that the Stewards
of the Jockey Club should have required an explanation of her
former bad running.

It was sticks and stones to Cunliffe. Amid the celebrations at Druid's
Lodge, he asked Fallon how was the health of Arthur Hamblin, the
commission agent? 'Very well, as far as I know,' replied Jack: 'Why?'
'Well,' drawled Cunliffe, 'It'd be a shame if he died before Monday
morning. We've £63,000 (*£5.9 million*) to come from him.' Jack
had been much less relaxed. 'Anxious? Of course I was. It was the
biggest thing I had ever attempted. For a fortnight before the race I
hardly slept.'

The Druid's Lodge coup over the 1903 Cambridgeshire has
consistently been reported down the years at £250,000. Today's
equivalent is a staggering £23 *million pounds*. The figure can't be
verified, of course. None of the Confederates would have dreamed
of broadcasting their winnings. Purefoy was at pains in later years to
talk down the scale of the coup.

The public who don't go racing much still imagine betting on a vast scale goes on, and for some reason or other, the belief is encouraged by a certain section of the Press, but it is not true. I believe I personally am credited with betting heavily, and if I stated the usual maximum of myself and my friends, it would be greeted with surprise and incredulity.

But Fallon did specify repeatedly that his own winnings were £32,000 (£3 million). Murray the stationmaster had £4,000 or £5,000 to come on his own account. If just one commission agent – albeit the main one – was delivering £63,000 to the stable's owners, then allowing for private commissions, for overseas winnings, and for Purefoy's countrywide punt, the £250,000 estimate might not be too far over the mark. Everyone was paid, too. Some of Murray's Midlands bookmaker victims asked for time, but got no sympathy. One paid £900 of a £2,000 liability on account. Suspecting a stopped cheque, Murray was outside the bank at opening time the next morning and sure enough, who should come along but the bookmaker. Little was said, but the cheque was met. Over in Ireland, Willie Rankin too had plenty to celebrate. He knew his filly, and he knew full well the hands into which he'd sold her. His own bets began with a £1,000 to £25.

One or two ordinary punters managed to penetrate the Confederates' smokescreen. There was the waiter at the Café Royal who told how one of his regular customers often talked to him about horses.

He came in about a fortnight before the Cambridgeshire and he gave me a horse. I think he told me about nearly every horse in the race on other occasions when he came in. Somebody said to me 'That gentleman is Mr Fallon who trains Hackler's Pride. Did he tell you anything?' Now

Hackler's Pride was the one horse he had never mentioned.
I thought it funny. I determined to take the plunge.

He drew out all his savings, lumped them on Hackler's Pride – and
bought his own hotel with the proceeds. The jockey Jack Jarvis
received a present of just £125. 'Not very liberal in view of what the
stable had won,' he remembered, 'but very nice for a boy of 15!'

From the advent of handicap racing, sharp owners and their
trainers have laid out horses to land betting coups. Winning a
Cambridgeshire with 6st 10lb doesn't represent the pinnacle of racing
excellence. If Hackler's Pride had never run another race she could
be assessed only as a useful tool for a hot stable. But events were to
show that she was up to, or close to, classic-winning standard in most
years. The Confederates may indeed not have known till later the full
strength of what they had up their sleeves that October afternoon at
Newmarket in 1903.

7.

Superhuman Cleverness

BESIDES THE JUBILEE and Cambridgeshire coups, the stable had two big-race wins in 1903 from Percy Cunliffe's Lord Rossmore. First, at Royal Ascot in the High-weight Stakes, then a fortnight later at the Curragh, where Lord Rossmore was made 6–4 favourite to beat a small field in the Irish Derby.

Lord Rossmore was off the bit virtually all the way. He didn't go the pace to half-way and was scrubbed along busily by Dillon. He made things harder still for himself by running wide into the straight, but eventually got home by a wafer-thin short head. Cunliffe ensured good reports for his colt by sending a case of champagne into the Press room. Lord Rossmore's wins sandwiched another major success for the apprentice Dillon. He was lent by Purefoy to his friend William I'Anson to partner Cliftonhall in the Northumberland Plate. The colt was backed to 2–1 and Ben steered him round Newcastle to win by five lengths.

After all the successes of the previous two seasons, it would have been no surprise if Druid's Lodge had a quiet time of it in 1904. Lady Luck – or the handicapper – would surely see to that. As it turned out, the coups of 1903 were simply a prelude to even greater rewards the following year. The first came right at the start of the flat, at Lincoln. It's a long time since the Carholme staged those annual curtain-raisers, the Brocklesby and the Lincolnshire Handicap. The course was flat and galloping, ideal for a big, long-striding horse, with no undue demands placed on suspect legs. Ideal, in fact, for Uninsured.

Hackler's Pride's runaway win at Newmarket had paid a healthy compliment to her galloping companions on Salisbury Plain, perhaps none more so than Frank Forester's home-bred Uninsured, by Laveno out of Surety. As a two year old, the bay gelding Uninsured was one of the stars of the Confederates' all-conquering 1902 season. He ran up a sequence of four wins in five weeks during October and November, all over five furlongs.

First, off the bottom of the handicap in a richly-endowed nursery at Kempton; then conceding weight all round in a maiden race at Sandown; then on to success in a handicap at Newmarket, where he beat several other previous winners; and finally Uninsured accompanied Hackler's Pride to Derby, where he gave weight away comfortably to eleven rivals in a maiden plate. His four wins earned Forester the tidy sum of £1,834 and since he started favourite each time, it's safe to assume that the bookmakers made additional contributions. Despite his profitable sequence, Uninsured had a suspicion of unsoundness, and Fallon thought him soft-hearted. But he was a big, lanky animal with a lot of racing as a two year old, and a lot of growing to do. The upshot was that he ran only three times as a three year old, never making the frame. He continued to show Fallon plenty on the gallops with Hackler's Pride in the autumn, though, and the trainer suggested to Forester that an early spring run against half-fit opponents at Lincoln might be just Uninsured's ticket.

After Christmas, Uninsured was put back into serious work,

again with Ypsilanti, Hackler's Pride and Lord Rossmore. It was
an unspeakably wet winter, affecting training grounds everywhere,
but the wonderful gallops at Druid's Lodge less than most. When
the Lincoln weights were published, there was Uninsured with the
highly satisfactory allotment of 7st 10lb. Purefoy and Cunliffe left
Fallon to the rain and wind on Salisbury Plain and sailed to South
Africa. There were plenty of bookmakers on the Rand offering
ante-post odds on the big English handicaps. What more could the
Confederates want than a bit of sunshine, a bit of business – and an
obliging bookmaker?

At the end of February, Uninsured stood at 100–7. Early in March,
Truth warned that 'All the sharps on the Turf are waiting eagerly for
Uninsured, and whenever the stable back this horse for a handicap
he is sure to start first favourite. The Lincoln course would suit
Uninsured very well if he could be got fit in time, and if the stable
commission could be executed.' Executed it certainly was, though
the week before the race *Truth* didn't 'See how the stable can have
backed him – so many people are looking out for the horse it'll be
difficult to execute a large commission at satisfactory odds.'

By the Monday of Lincoln week, Uninsured's odds had halved to
7–1 and *The Sporting Life* reported that 'At the eleventh hour he has
been supported to win a very large sum of money.' The *Life* had 'No
doubt that most of the early business emanated from South Africa.'
The final commission was simultaneously worked by Purefoy all over
the country. On the morning of the race Uninsured was backed to
9–2 clear favourite. His preparation hadn't been entirely worry-free:
Fallon fretted that he might have given the gelding one gallop too
many. Uninsured sported eye-catching blue bandages in the parade
at Lincoln. But the weather had taken its toll on his opponents'
preparation. Few of the 23 runners looked fully wound up. Among his
main rivals, Lord Marcus Beresford's Cerisier was widely reckoned

thrown in with just 6st 6lb – and 5lb to come off when a young apprentice was engaged.

At flag-fall Cerisier set off as if the hounds of hell were at his heels. His closest companion at half-way was Wolfshall, the easy winner of a £500 Hurst Park handicap the previous May, and representing another formidable South African connection, Harry Barnato. But Uninsured was close up and going well under Ben Dillon. Two furlongs out, Cerisier's boy picked up his whip, and the colt at once veered away. Wolfshall hit the front, but in the last hundred yards Uninsured took his measure, winning readily by three-quarters of a length. Cerisier ran on to be beaten two lengths back in fourth.

The reception given to Uninsured was surprisingly cordial. As *Truth* had forecast, every shrewdie on the racecourse was on the look-out. It was just a question as to where the horse was 'slipped'. *The Sporting Life*, having recommended Uninsured for weeks, was bursting with approval: 'the cleverest handicap stable in the Kingdom has scored once more.' 'It is astonishing what few mistakes this stable makes, and after sitting for a season like Patience on a monument they have made the Ring pay for gazing at the pose.'

Sometimes, of course, there can be unpleasant sequels. When a horse sporting a fine row of duck-eggs in the form book suddenly swoops in and carries off a big handicap with every sign in the betting of being 'expected,' aspersions can be cast. Stewards can enquire. But all that happened on the Carholme was an aggrieved punter yelling 'There go the bloody cheats!' as Forester and the others led Uninsured from the winning enclosure. With £3 *million* and more to come in winnings, it's to be supposed that they didn't very much care.

A fortnight later, the Confederates were at Kempton, to watch Ypsilanti's seasonal debut under 9st in the £1,325-to-the-winner Queen's Prize. Ypsilanti was 11–4 second favourite, backed down from 5–1. He looked exceptionally well in the parade – further evidence that the Druid's Lodge team had come through the winter better than most, and he won without turning a hair. Held up off the pace, he burst through below the distance to win, eased at the finish, by four lengths and three from good handicappers, conceding them lumps of weight.

Ypsilanti then went to Lingfield for an exercise canter in a five-runner apprentice race, with long odds heavily laid on, before tackling the Jubilee again early in May. He was already becoming a favourite with the Kempton crowd, but sentiment had to be tempered by realism. Ypsilanti had a 10lb penalty for his win in the Queen's Prize, bringing his weight to a crushing 9st 5lb. The obvious dangers included L'Aiglon – receiving almost two stones, and easy winner of a big handicap at Sandown – and the Lincoln fourth, Cerisier, carrying just 5st 13lb.

Through Uninsured and others, the Confederates had precise lines to Ypsilanti's chance against Cerisier. Those lines convinced Purefoy that the chance was small to non-existent. He not only threw in for a big win over Cerisier; he laid Ypsilanti to all comers. 'The horse is very fit,' Fallon told Purefoy: 'I think he's certain to win.' Pure looked at Jack with an expression compounded of pity and calculation. 'How much are you having on him?' he asked. 'A couple of hundred for now,' replied Jack. Pure laid the bet while Frank Forester listened intently; he too had the odds to £200. Some friends in the group were obliged and for good measure, Pure stuck the stable lads' bets as well.

Pure wasn't the only one to field against the previous year's winner. Lord Marcus Beresford had offered to buy Ypsilanti after the Queen's Prize, with the idea of sending him to race in India,. Cunliffe named £2,500 as his price. On the morning of the Jubilee, Beresford sent his vet Leach to look Ypsilanti over. The dodgy leg was no secret, and it wasn't stopping the horse from better and better weight-carrying performances, but Leach just couldn't bring himself to ignore it. Fallon told him he was looking at the Jubilee winner. The vet examined the swelling, shook his head, and clearly thought Fallon was mad. 'All right,' said Jack, 'you'll see: nobody knows how good this horse is. Take my advice and back him.' Disbelieving, Leach went off to tell Beresford that it was absurd to think of buying the horse.

Even setting the infirmity aside, most of the professionals shared Purefoy's opinion that Ypsilanti had too much weight to win his second Jubilee. But the good judges at least saved on him, with the result that he came from 100–8 to 100–12 in the betting. L'Aiglon was a strong favourite at 3–1, despite racecourse rumour that he'd broken loose at exercise and gone for a long solo gallop that morning. L'Aiglon came round the Sunbury bend in a clear lead, and looked home and hosed two furlongs out. Just as his backers started to count their winnings, he stopped as if shot – racecourse rumour was justified, for once – and Ypsilanti and Cerisier hit the front together. After a sharp struggle on the run to the line, Ypsilanti – conceding 48lb – proved the stronger, winning by three-quarters of a length.

There were some anxious moments in the unsaddling enclosure. Cerisier had the rails all the way up the straight, and with Dillon riding vigorously with his whip in his left hand, many thought his mount had tightened up Cerisier. But the runner-up's connections refused to lay an objection, and the 'All Right' was cheered to the echo. Purefoy took his reverse sportingly: 'I think it is the only race I ever felt glad to lose money on, and felt as glad when he won as if I had won a packet myself.'

For Pure at least, there'd be other days and other winnings to come with Ypsilanti. The feelings of Lord Beresford – not to mention 'Boss' Croker – can be imagined when the one-time selling plater and supposed cripple went through the 1904 season in England unbeaten. He walked over in the Rothschild Plate at Manchester, gave the Cesarewitch winner Wargrave a hammering at Hurst Park, and then walked over for another Rothschild Plate, this time at Windsor. His only defeat was in Paris, on that black Sunday in October when Pretty Polly, in appalling ground and after a rough Channel crossing, was beaten into second place in the Prix du Conseil Municipal by an unconsidered outsider, with Lord Howard de Walden's Zinfandel third. Not surprisingly, the London papers concentrated their Longchamp reports on Pretty Polly, producing memorably chauvinistic headlines like *The Sporting Life's* 'A French horse wins. Pretty Polly beats Zinfandel.'

But Ypsilanti was a desperately unlucky loser, beaten three-quarters of a length and the same in a six-horse race for the Prix de Newmarket. He conceded between 11lb and 42lb to his rivals, and Dillon rode a stinker. The English contingent at Longchamp had a rare gamble on Ypsilanti, anticipating playing up their winnings on Pretty Polly later, and he was sent off the 4–7 favourite. One Northern professional, Tom Barrasford, lost £16,000 over Ypsilanti in Paris: a small matter of *a million and a half* today.

The chagrin of 'Boss' and Lord Beresford was prolonged by Ypsilanti for another two seasons. In 1905 he won four more races. First a £350 plate at Warwick in April, where with 4–11 laid on, he all but pulled his jockey out of the saddle in beating a solitary opponent by six lengths. He won another match at Kempton later in the month, at the prohibitive odds of 1–20, and then bid for his third successive Jubilee. The handicapper hadn't taken the remotest chance this time. Ypsilanti carried 9st 13lb. None the less, he was backed from 12–1 to 5–1 ante-post. He looked magnificent in the paddock – 'He needs to, with all that weight,' muttered William Jarvis – and was so full of beans in the parade that his saddle slipped. Purefoy adjusted matters on the course in front of the Members' enclosure, and when the old horse finally cantered down to the start the crowd along the rails cheered him all the way. There was no fairy-tale result. Ypsilanti started slowly, and lost ground at the bend after some scrimmaging. He eventually finished eleventh of the 14 runners.

After a short break, Ypsilanti went to Lewes for an exercise canter in a £350 plate. He frightened off all but one opponent, and won by 15 lengths at 1–66, before dishing out another thrashing – 9 lb and 20 lengths – to his old foe Wargrave at Hurst Park. He ran only four times in 1906, winning just a little race at Windsor in the autumn. 'Poor old Ypsilanti got to be looked on as a has-been, yet he was as sound and good as ever,' wrote Purefoy. He just 'got rather sick of carrying about 9st 7lb in handicaps and seeing some light-weight with 6st jump off and keep him on the stretch all the way.'

After Windsor, the Confederates sold Ypsilanti to stud in Canada. Including his initial win in that Hurst Park seller, he won 16 times. He earned Cunliffe £10,090 in win and place money. He won the most valuable and hotly-contested handicap in England twice, landing thumping gambles – not to mention a useful place stake in the Lincoln. All that on 'three good legs and a swinger.' At 420 guineas, has there ever been a better buy out of a selling plate?

Ypsilanti's second Jubilee success had been preceded by a set-back in April in the City and Suburban when Hackler's Pride was well fancied in a field of 21. She handled the descent into the Epsom straight badly and though she moved into a challenging position for a stride or two below the distance, she backpedalled rapidly in the final furlong. Also, as the result of her smashing win at Newmarket, she'd been transformed from a flyweight into top weight. The Confederates promptly put her away till the autumn, and she reappeared in a mile handicap at Doncaster on the day that Pretty Polly won the St Leger. Hackler's Pride again had top weight, and shared favouritism, but she finished at the back of the 10-runner field.

Three days later, *The Winning Post* cast its eye over the long-range prospects for the 1904 Cambridgeshire, and concluded that 'Hackler's Pride must have extinguished all hope of winning this race for the second year in succession by her performance on Town Moor.' The alternative explanation – that here was an autumn filly having a quiet prep race after a 21 week absence – was, though, advanced by the same paper's betting correspondent a week later: 'The astute Fallon's stable must always be respected, no matter what may be the look or outside estimate of their horses.'

The Cambridgeshire weights were headed by Pretty Polly with 9st. 2lb. On 9st were the much-travelled top French four-year-old Caius (winner of what are now Group races at Deauville, Longchamp, Chantilly and Baden-Baden) and the prolific big-handicap winner Union Jack. On 8st 10lb came Hackler's Pride, Peter Purcell Gilpin's Delaunay – the unbeaten winner of 11 races; and another of Gilpin's, the Yorkshire Oaks winner Hammerkop. Buried away among the 51 entries was another from Druid's Lodge, Frank Forester's Golden Saint, and two of Lord Carnarvon's with an authentic handicap 'feel' about them, Laveuse and Vril.

At the first call-overs in mid-September, Hackler's Pride began as she had the previous year – at 33–1. Within a week she was down to 20–1, whereupon the Confederates repeated their pea-and-thimble ruse and began backing Golden Saint. The three year old was impossible to assess – unraced as a two year old and then the winner of little races at Gatwick and Warwick, the second by six lengths. But with just 6st 8lb to carry, the bookmakers imagined Golden Saint might be anything. He was cut from 25–1 to 100–7 in the last week of September, with the result that Hackler's Pride was extended once more to 25–1. That was the signal for Purefoy to get stuck in. In no time at all Hackler's Pride was down to 10–1. There were two other big commissions circulating, though, for Delaunay and Caius, with the result that fractions up to 100–7 were freely available about Hackler's Pride for the next 10 days. Bob Denman, the Chantilly-based English trainer of Caius, predicted freely that Caius would win. There were no 'ifs' – connections regarded him as a good thing.

The other significant market move was for the Whatcombe hope, Laveuse. But no sooner had the betting public cottoned on, than Laveuse was withdrawn. The explanation which filtered out of Whatcombe was that Lord Carnarvon 'had been unable to find a suitable jockey.' The reality, said the cynics, was that he was enraged at being forestalled in the market. So Vril was left as the sole standard-bearer for Whatcombe. Meanwhile, Hackler's Pride was giving every satisfaction on the Druid's Lodge gallops. She'd been plagued with a sore mouth, but the removal of three teeth cured that, and the local touts hailed her as 'improving daily.'

The Winning Post, which had tipped Delaunay at 25–1, none the less warned that Hackler's Pride 'is as fit as it's possible to make her, and fully justifies her position in the market.' In the last few days before the race she was whittled steadily down to 7–1. No one could claim that they hadn't been warned. 'Double P' Gilpin said that 'I don't think much of the mare with 8st 10lb – but I think a lot of the people!' In its final review of the race, The Winning Post wrote that:

> Last year's winner Hackler's Pride, the property of Captain
> Forester, has been a medium of a great plunge and should
> she repeat her victory of last year will take more money out
> of the Ring than was the case then. A good mare with plenty
> of speed, and stamina for the distance well proved, she must
> be put down as a most dangerous candidate, if not the most,
> and hailing from the stable governed by such master minds
> in handicap racing as those of Mr Purefoy, Mr A. P. Cunliffe
> and last but not least Fallon. The stable make few mistakes if

any in big races when they plank their money down as they
have here.

And plank it down Purefoy certainly did. On the eve of the race the
Pride was 7 to 1. On the day, she was backed down to joint favourite
with Caius at 7–2, Delaunay was 5–1, and Carnarvon's second string
Vril was a strong 100–8 chance. It was a beautiful day. The going was
perfect. A big French contingent had travelled over to cheer home
Caius. Hackler's Pride was again late into the parade, and again
her outstanding condition caught the eye. As luck would have it,
Jack Fallon was at the paddock exit alongside Caius's master, Bob
Denman. 'God, whose is that?' blurted Denman, as Hackler's Pride
tore past him to the start. 'Mine,' smiled Fallon. Denman pushed into
the Ring for a £50 saver.

Ben Dillon had the filly quickest away of the 17 runners, and she
led to half-way. Headed briefly by two of the lightweights, she was
fairly rousted up by Dillon and led again at the Bushes. Close behind,
Caius lost his action going down into the dip, and Vril came out
along with Delaunay to throw down the last and biggest challenge.
Under the strongest imaginable driving from Dillon, Hackler's Pride
never flinched for a stride. Delaunay's 11 wins had all been at up to
a mile, and the last incline found him out. Vril, receiving 30lb, but
a crucial 1lb overweight, was wearing Hackler's Pride down at the
finish, but was still a neck behind at the post. The 1902 third, Nabot
ran on to be third again, half a length back. The high-class Delaunay
and Caius were fourth and fifth. To frank the form, the previously
unbeaten Delaunay promptly won his next three races in 1904 – and
three out of four in 1905. Caius won five major races the following
year.

Hackler's Pride's win was not only supremely game but, unlike the
previous year, it was genuinely popular, particularly since it frustrated

what was regarded as deplorable behaviour by Carnarvon with Laveuse and Vril. *The Sporting Life* sounded a rare hostile note:

> Her victory, gamely though it was obtained, could not in the nature of things be so popular as that of Delaunay or Caius would have been, the contrast between her running at Epsom and Doncaster with what she accomplished yesterday being very marked.

Robert Sievier in *The Winning Post* had no reservations: 'The Cambridgeshire was a great race, and the quality of the field above average.' Paying the highest compliment he knew, Sievier wrote that 'Hackler's Pride is more of a machine than a racehorse, and is nearer a likeness to Sceptre than any other horse in training.' He had some hard words for Whatcombe:

> That Lord Carnarvon threw the race away by the scratching of Laveuse is the general opinion of the man in the street, and this person adds that this was done out of pique, someone more or less connected with the stable having stepped into the market and backed her. One thing is certain, that if Laveuse is two lengths better than Vril, which report had was so, then indeed the Cambridgeshire has been left behind. Two more strides and Vril must have beaten the fading-away heroine of the day.

'The Druid's Lodge stable have landed a great coup; one of the biggest this establishment has ever succeeded in winning,' concluded Sievier, who knew a thing or two about coups. 'It was always difficult to back Hackler's Pride, and the several commission agents of the stable refused nothing.'

It was left to *Truth* to disturb the celebrations at Druid's Lodge. The paper hailed Hackler's Pride as 'The best four year old in training. Defeating Caius, Delaunay and Nabot at the weights was better than the very tip top of handicap form. It is greatly to be regretted that Hackler's Pride was not engaged in last year's classic stakes.' But there was a sting:

> Her running has certainly not been remarkable for consistency, for usually her performances have been exceedingly moderate, but her victory in each season has been achieved when the stable money has been fairly piled upon her. Captain Forester has been very lucky in connecting himself with a stable that is managed with an almost superhuman cleverness.

Forester was enraged. He sent the offending comments to the Jockey Club, with the demand that they examine the running of his horses. He was looking for exoneration; he hardly got what he expected.

8.

Celebrities in Glass Houses

IN EVERY WAY possible, the 1904 season surpassed the Confederates' wildest dreams. They landed spectacular gambles in three of the flat's most valuable handicaps, and they also exacted tribute from the bookies in numerous lesser events. Typical was the June afternoon when Fallon took three horses to Gatwick. Percy Cunliffe's two year old Shanid-a-Boo was backed from 5–1 to half those odds to win a five-furlong maiden. The next race was a most peculiar event – a £1,000 (£94,000) selling handicap. The fourteen runners were briefly '7–1 the field' before Purefoy's Orphrey was backed to 4–1 clear favourite. He won easily, and was sold afterwards for 550 guineas. In the next race Edward Wigan's Lapsang (6–4 from 2–1) completed the gambled-on Druid's Lodge and Ben Dillon treble. And so it went on. The season's tally of 37 winners might have fallen a few short of 1902, but the win prize money was a new peak: £14,758. Everything seemed roses. Cunliffe was entertaining hugely at Druid's Lodge. Its 50-foot drawing room was tailor-made for parties. He had 11 bedrooms to accommodate house parties from London, and Pure supplied the sparkle in the shape of theatre world personalities – and some of the girls from his shows.

At the end of the flat season, it was time for shooting, and there were few better places in Britain for crack shots like Purefoy, Forester and Wigan to enjoy their sport. Edward Wigan negotiated to buy another great shooting estate, the beautiful Conholt Park, a few miles away near Andover. And when the hunting season began, Forester was out regularly with the Wilton. After the pack ran riot in the crops of the vicar at nearby Durrington, Forester donated a new organ to the parish church. Mind you, the vicar was the giant, ill-tempered Parson Parkes – occasional owner and trainer of bad horses, and infinitely better known for his fists than his sermons – so possibly Forester was only being prudent.

That December, Forester and the Confederates had two unwelcome intrusions to their entertainments. First was the Jockey Club's reply to Forester's complaint about *Truth* and its innuendos. It came at the Gimcrack dinner in York, from Lord Durham, the senior steward of the Jockey Club. Durham had made a name for himself as a young man seventeen years earlier, when at the same historic dinner he sensationally attacked the conduct of a fellow member of the Jockey Club, Sir George Chetwynd, and his Newmarket trainer:

> There is a well known and aristocratic racing stable that
> has been conspicuous throughout the racing season for the
> constant and inexplicable in-and-out running of its horses.
> Their running has surprised and disgusted the public, besides
> losing them their money. It has driven the handicappers to
> their wits' end to discover the true form of the horses they
> have to apportion weights to, and it has scandalised all true
> lovers of the sport of horse racing.

In December of 1904, still filled with fire and brimstone, Durham
launched into the racing Press. According to the report of his speech,
he 'Was glad to think there were some unbiased and independent
writers amongst us, but they were fast diminishing in numbers. [He]
was astonished how the editors of sporting newspapers can possibly
print the ridiculous rubbish that is sent to them.' He then turned to
handicappers and handicapping. The report read:

> Handicappers were bound to impose such weights as were
> justified by a horse's public performances and he did think
> that when handicappers had satisfied themselves that some
> owner had run his horse improperly and had thereby gained
> an advantage over an honest owner, then the handicapper was
> perfectly justified in imposing not only upon that horse, but
> any horse belonging to the same owner, a prohibitive weight.

Few of his audience needed any prompting to know who he had
in mind. The most charitable explanation of his fantastic suggestion
was implied by *The Winning Post*, where Bob Sievier wrote: 'We
are told by the Chief of the Turf *after dinner admittedly*...' But the
Confederates would find the following season that Durham was by
no means speaking in his cups.

A fortnight later, from the opposite end of the racing
establishment, it was Sievier himself who called attention to Druid's
Lodge in a way that was as damning as Durham's. Sievier had
launched *The Winning Post* (price one penny: 'a Bob for a penny,'
called the newsboys) in August 1904, at the tail end of one of his
innumerable lawsuits and after being warned off. It was a great
success. Within three months it was selling over 128,000 copies a
week. Its popularity was based on risqué jokes, cunning cartoons,
society tittle-tattle – and superlative racing coverage. Aspects of

all four were contained in a full-page feature entitled *Celebrities in Glass Houses*. The feature was signed each week by Tweedledum and Tweedledee – a Sievier *nom de plume*. *Celebrities* expanded over the years to encompass politicians, touring cricket teams, The New Year and all sorts. But in the early issues of *The Winning Post*, the feature concentrated on racing personalities.

To Percy Cunliffe's horror, on Christmas Eve he was the Celebrity. Over breakfast in his rooms in the fashionable Albany apartments off Piccadilly, he found himself addressed as:

Mr A. P. Cunliffe
of Druid's Lodge

Sir

We hope you are quite well, as this leaves us at present.

We have been tempted almost irresistibly to address you many times before this, but after struggling with our feelings we have saved you for Christmas. What could have been more appropriate for this season of goodwill towards men, or more wholesome?

With us it is now the most charitable time of the year, and on this count alone we claim your indulgence, as we on our part assure you of ours, even to the superlative. To at once demonstrate our meaning can we say more than you are Tweedledum and Tweedledee's Christmas card? We dish you up as seasonable fare, at a time when the world should be merry and gay, placing you in our gallery bedecked with holly, not forgetting a sprig of mistletoe – for the latter has from time immemorial been emblematic of the Druids from whom your racing establishment takes its name.

No stable is better known to the public by name than
is Druid's Lodge, and as the reigning priest of this the
best-appointed place of its kind in England, you are to be
congratulated. Envied you have been often, but you can afford
to pass these human foibles by, for envy has caused even
angels to fall, and what has been will be again. It is said of
your stable that it has been successful even to astonishment,
and the handicap results added up would come out as a sum
total in the one word 'genius.'

Nor have recent events made the kudos of this
unique state of things any the less, for your honesty and
straightforwardness has been fully endorsed by the authorities.
Have we not been recently told in a public speech that any
owner – and we presume stable – not running a horse in that
satisfactory sporting fashion pleasing to the handicapper,
the lot – lock, stock, and barrel – shall be secretly mulcted
with prohibitive weights. Hence your many achievements in
handicaps is a most satisfactory certificate of the esteem with
which the stewards and officials hold your stable.

As the late Duke of Westminster was respected – might we
not say beloved? – as the 'classic' of the Turf, so can we look
upon Druid's Lodge in the same light regarding handicaps,
with help of the official diction we have referred to rising up
before us. The quintessence of our remarks comes to this: there
is not a single handicapper – and today his verdict appears
more vital than the judge's – who has ever raised a finger
against your honour, or the consistency of your horses. We
accept the verdict so practically pronounced and throwing
Ruff's Guide among the Christmas logs think no more of it.

Your official popularity is doubtless well earned, and you
have our hearty congratulations. If in the fullness of time it

ever becomes a Royal fashion to bestow upon owners those gracious and distinguished honours which on auspicious and rare occasions are conferred in other walks of life, a peerage would indeed be yours: while amongst trainers and we except neither John Porter nor Richard Marsh, Fallon might without disappointment expect the right to add a few distinguishing letters to his name, the choosing of which might be left to the public by way of being able to express its appreciation.

That you are one of the most level-headed of owners is common knowledge, while hidden beneath your solidity of character there lurks a dry humour, subtly cynical and smart. As an instance, on the morning of the recent Cambridgeshire one of your stable rushed up all exuberance and spirit, informing you with increased confidence, if such were necessary, that he had vividly dreamt that Hackler's Pride had won. Unconcerned, without a smile on those features which are peculiarly your own, you inquired, 'Indeed, what were second and third?'

The richest owner you have among you at Druid's Lodge is, we would venture to suggest, Captain Forester. True to the traditions which enshrine Druid's Lodge, his horses have seldom attempted and never gained classic honours, while on the other hand he has won a lucky-bag full of handicaps. These successes since recent enlightenment must stand out in the front rank of Turf honours, for whereas the 'prohibited' owner can continue his sweet way with guileless pleasure in classic and weight-for-age races unmolested by the adjuster of weights, handicaps can only be won through the channel of honesty and straightforward and consistent running, intersprinkled with the glorious uncertainty of the Turf – to an accepted degree. The degree is a matter for the officials.

We heartily ejaculate, 'More power to your elbow!' True,
the present position of things brings us to a state of topsy-
turvydom, for while a dishonest owner can walk off with
the Derby, St Leger or, for that matter, the whole five classics,
he would be 'prohibited' from winning the most trumpery
of selling handicaps. This enhances your surroundings and
your elaborately successful policy. It must now be accepted
that the highest honours of the Turf are associated with
victory in a big handicap, the owners running being under
rigid observation and secret control. Weighing these matters,
what could be more satisfactory than two [victories] in the
Cambridgeshire in succession with the same animal! This your
stable did, and it speaks for itself. For a man to win a handicap
is for him to be publicly franked with the official seal and
Druid's Lodge is continually receiving this gratifying mark.

Apart from these official qualifications, it can be
said of you that you have never once misled any of your
acquaintances by imparting to them incorrect information.
In fact, so securely have you safeguarded yourself against
this pitfall, that we cannot find a solitary individual to
whom you have ever discussed anything in the way of
'Druidical' advice. This displays your forethought, for
though at times your prophecies might have borne pecuniary
fruit, once let them fail and the opposite result drowns all
else. When you have had prospectively successful horses
running in a race, we have even seen you meander out of
the club enclosure and mix with the crowd in Tattersall's
ring, avoiding those pestering inquirers who might have
no shadow of right to address you, and under ordinary
circumstances could not claim more than a 'How-do-you-do!'
acquaintanceship.

We are positive, so far as the glorious uncertainty will permit, that you would have been ever ready to tell anyone your stable secrets if it were certain not to make any possible difference to you. What more can these people expect of an owner?! You will agree with us they are all too unreasonable, expecting everything and giving nothing. The mere fact that Druid's Lodge is running a horse in a handicap should in itself be sufficient, and why the public, or any of their number, should express a curiosity as to this or that concerning it, is really too unutterably silly, is it not? Though you might be described as a man without a smile, you nevertheless must often inwardly chuckle to yourself, and laugh that guffaw of satisfaction which, though not marked in every feature, tickles all your thoughts.

You must have at your command a marvellous faculty, for the way your commissions have been engineered deserves all commercial recommendations and would vie with the ingenuity of Throgmorton Street, or, to be more pointed, Threadneedle Street. To add to this accomplishment your dry humour in these transactions often asserts itself, and what could have been more apropos as a set-off to Hackler's Pride than the confusion caused in the market by a Golden Saint! The seer who named this colt was indeed far-seeing. Hackler's Pride was in substance the Golden Saint, yet it was the phantom golden saint that secured the price about Hackler's Pride!

To enumerate the horses located at Druid's Lodge, and to recapitulate their many handicap successes, would fill our pages, and though you have not yet achieved anything in particular that goes to make Turf history, it can be written of your stable that the three owners who go to make up the ruling triumvirate of its destinies can be described under the following three headings – Croesus, St Patrick, and Job.

Your obedient servants,

TWEEDLEDUM AND TWEEDLEDEE

After this biting and revealing sarcasm, the Confederates' discomfiture was increased in March when Purefoy too received the doubtful compliment of an appearance in *Celebrities in Glass Houses*. Pure was wickedly cartooned as 'Sporting and Burlesque', wearing his racing colours above a dancer's tutu, crowned with a 'halo' fashioned from a riding crop. 'The reason for your success,' he was advised by Tweedledum and Tweedledee, is 'stringently adhering to the Druid's Lodge motto that Silence is Golden. The discretion you have shown in the manipulation of your commissions is the envy of the less ingenious.' Sievier completed a hat-trick of highly public digs at the Confederates with The Snark's full-page cartoon of the trapped bookie and the punter who interfered, captioned, *'To be taken in connection with our letter to Mr A. P. Cunliffe.'*

Meanwhile, Druid's Lodge was learning that Lord Durham's signals were indeed being heeded by the handicappers. Ypsilanti and Hackler's Pride were both set to carry over 9st in the 1905 Lincoln – with the bottom weights on 6st 2lb – but though an effort of sorts was made to promote Hackler's Pride as ante-post favourite, not a penny of the backing came from the Confederates. Ypsilanti was left in the race up to the last minute, but this time the Salisbury Plain pea in the thimble was in a neighbouring yard, John Powney's revived Grateley. With no serious aspirations for their own entries, Fallon and Pure allowed Powney to try his hope Rosebury against Hackler's Pride. Rosebury was weighted as for the Lincoln – which was to say receiving 3st – and he won the gallop well. In a race made absurd by the absence of the Druid's Lodge horses the top weight carried 7st 10lb, and 11 of the 18 runners were below 7st. Third-favourite Rosebury dented plenty of pockets by running nowhere. Ironically, the winner was Sansovin, beaten out of sight by Hackler's Pride in the Cambridgeshire, and only 2lb better off with her at Lincoln.

The oddest feature of an odd race was that one of the unplaced brigade, Vedas, by Florizel II out of Agnostic, went on from carrying 6st 3lb at Lincoln (and finishing a poor ninth) to win the 2,000 Guineas. The assumption that this must have been the biggest fluke or the worst classic of all time has to be balanced by the fact that the Guineas second, Signorina, beaten two lengths, was later beaten only a length for the Derby. Whatever fanciful handicapping calculations all this might produce, they weren't likely to be favourable to Hackler's Pride. Nor were they. From time to time she was entered for a major handicap for a look at the weights, but what Forester saw wasn't encouraging. So she went pot-hunting – a walk-over at Kempton followed by a win by a distance at 1–50 in a match at Salisbury. Then she was given 9st 6lb in the Hunt Cup, and was scratched at once. She found an easier route to Ascot success in the two-runner Rous Memorial Stakes, which she duly won by five lengths at 1–25. She enjoyed another walk-over at Salisbury before being beaten under 12st 2lb in a ten-furlong gentleman's race for Bibury Club members, where a high-class hurdler outstayed her. Hackler's Pride then failed narrowly to give lumps of weight away in handicaps at Kempton and Doncaster.

Thoughts of a Cambridgeshire hat-trick were dashed when the weights for the autumn double were published. Hackler's Pride was not only given 9st 7lb; she was weighted punitively. Nabot, for example, could be measured pretty exactly with her from the 1904 race. He'd been a neck and half a length behind her, receiving 4lb, yet he was set to receive 13lb now: 9lb for three parts of a length. It was the

"SPORT AND BURLESQUE."

Wilfred Purefoy lampooned by *The Winning Post* as 'Sports and Burlesque', reference to his interests in both racing and music hall theatre.

same story with other Druid's Lodge entries in the Cambridgeshire and Cesarewitch. In a long assessment of the weights for the two races, Sievier showed in *The Winning Post* how with horse after horse, the Druid's Lodge contingent were up to 10lb more harshly treated at Newmarket than in earlier handicaps at Doncaster – despite all of them, Hackler's Pride included, having run unplaced. Sievier speculated that the Committee of Handicappers 'Has received some kind of semi-official intimation on the basis which Lord Durham proclaimed in his speech at the Gimcrack dinner.'

Never one to pass up a chance to create some mischief, Sievier described the weights allotted to Hackler's Pride, Lady Drake and Queen's Holiday as:

A slur upon the running of Captain Forester's horses – indeed, the whole of the Druid's Lodge horses. Surely it devolves on him to call on the handicappers for an explanation. If Captain Forester does not take the matter up, and leaves it where it stands, then he must accept the critical comments which are likely to be passed upon his silence.

Forester, having had no satisfaction the previous time he'd complained to the racing authorities, had no intention of starting any public wrangle. He was furious, but he was also a realist. There were no more big handicaps to be won with Hackler's Pride. So when a prominent breeder came along with a £5,000 offer for her, he let her go, with the proviso that she stayed at Druid's Lodge while she remained in training.

Hackler's Pride's new owner was Sir Tatton Sykes, a legendary recluse and eccentric with a huge estate at Sledmere in the Yorkshire Wolds. His passions included restoring ruined churches and eating milk puddings. He had a large stud of mostly indifferent bloodstock.

Hackler's Pride was the intended foundation mare for a new dynasty. She carried the seldom-seen Sykes colours – orange with purple sleeves – three times, all at Newmarket, before retiring. First, over seven furlongs, when she received weight-for-sex from her Cambridgeshire foe Nabot, and gave just 1lb to the three year old Vedas. She beat them both easily, Nabot by three lengths, with the 2,000 Guineas winner a further five lengths back. A fortnight later Hackler's Pride put up the best performance of her career, in defeat, in the Champion Stakes. It was a two-runner race, and the other was Pretty Polly. On the face of it, the race was a mismatch – a top handicapper up against one of the greatest race mares of all time, at level weights.

Pretty Polly's achievements hardly need retelling. She came to the Champion Stakes the winner of 17 of her 18 starts, including the 1,000 Guineas, Oaks and St Leger of 1904. Still, at the start of the 1905 season, Bob Sievier, in hailing Hackler's Pride as 'One of the most brilliant mares we have seen for some time,' pondered that 'with all Pretty Polly's brilliancy we are even inclined to question which is the best of the two – though we should favour the classic winner.' In the Champion Stakes match, they bet 2–5 Pretty Polly. Not only was she already recognised as a phenomenon ('I have never seen such a filly in all my experience of the Turf,' wrote the celebrated 'Special Commissioner' of *The Sportsman*, William Allison): there was a widespread assumption that Hackler's Pride was a miler who by handicapping, superb training and her own courage had just got nine furlongs twice, and certainly wouldn't get 10 against Pretty Polly. So it proved. Ben Dillon jumped her off smartly, and she led Pretty Polly at a good clip across the flat. At the Bushes, with both mares ridden along, Dillon still had her a length and a half to the good. In the Dip, she tired visibly, and swerved. By contrast, Danny Maher had Pretty Polly stretching out supremely well, and she went away easily to win by two lengths. 'I do not think Pretty Polly has ever been seen to much greater advantage,' wrote one observer.

The two mares and their jockeys returned to a tremendous reception. There needn't be any excuses for Hackler's Pride. She was beaten comfortably. But to run beyond her own best trip and still be beaten only two lengths by Pretty Polly (who won all her three classics by further) was a performance good enough to claim a classic for herself in most years. It would have to have been the 1,000 Guineas, since she only just got nine furlongs. Jack Fallon had no doubts on that score: 'At up to a mile, she would have been a match, and more, for Sceptre and for Pretty Polly.'

Happily, Hackler's Pride ended her racing days on a winning note. Despite finishing the Champion Stakes exhausted, she was pulled out the following afternoon to face two opponents in the one-mile Select Stakes. One of them, on the same terms as a fortnight earlier, was the unfortunate Nabot, who must by this time have been heartily sick of Hackler's Pride. They ran the same race; Hackler's Pride made all, pulling double, and won in a canter. Nabot was two lengths second. So ended one of the most lucrative racing careers of the twentieth century. She won two Cambridgeshires and five other races for the Confederates, and two more for Sir Tatton Sykes. She won the equivalent of *half a million pounds* in prize money; but she also won Druid's Lodge perhaps as much as *£30 million* in bets. She had a long and contented time in the paddocks at Sledmere. She lived to the ripe old age of 22, and produced 14 foals from 17 coverings. Her yearlings generally fetched good prices in the sale ring, and half of them won. She bred the winners Brancepeth, Sobieski, Torchbearer (USA), Gift of the Gab, Ionian, Free From Pride and Thracia. None of them, alas, was half as good as she was.

9.

The Best Two Year Old in the World

THE FOUR WINS that Hackler's Pride recorded before being sold contributed to another marvellous year for the Confederates. Fallon trained 39 winners for them in 1905, netting £14,955 in win prizes. But at the end of the season, tensions at Druid's Lodge surfaced in public. In August, *Sporting Sketches* noted that it had long been foreseen:

That the shortness of money brought about by the war
in South Africa would have its effect upon the Turf. Rumours
are afloat that the sport is about to lose some of its most
prominent patrons. We believe that the dangerous and
skilfully managed Druid's Lodge will exist no longer – at
any rate under its present auspices – after the present season.'

Besides external factors like the Boer War, there were domestic problems at Druid's Lodge. *The Sporting Life* speculated in October that Jack Fallon could soon be leaving, and that another local trainer,

Tommy Lewis, would take his place. Jack had had enough. True, the discipline at Druid's Lodge wasn't as harsh as in the early days, but why tolerate the tedious nights on Salisbury Plain when he was now a rich man? Bernard Dillon too was restless. He was getting some prime outside rides, not least for P. P. Gilpin's Newmarket stable, and cutting a swathe through the chorus girls on his rare free nights in London. But on the gallops in the early spring of 1906, there was a powerful incentive for Jack to buckle down for one last season's employment at Druid's Lodge. The incentive was a colt of Purefoy's called Lally.

Lally's rise and fall and rise was to tax Purefoy's iron nerve to breaking point, win and lose fortunes in bets, and bring about Fallon's departure. From his days as a foal at Greenfields, the home-bred chestnut was the apple of Purefoy's eye. He was by a Hardwicke Stakes winner, Amphion, out of Miss Hoyden, the £54 buy at Tattersalls in 1896. Pure named Lally after a favourite actress, Lily Elsie. Years later, despite Lally's part in his downfall, Fallon still hailed the colt as 'probably the best animal that ever came through my hands'.

When Lally made his debut in a four-furlong Sandown maiden at the end of April 1905, it was an educational outing. He started at 8–1, and his jockey Bert Lynham was under instructions not to touch him. Lally started slowly and ran on strongly into third. He started favourite for his next eight races, and won six of them. In betting terms, Lally was the least 'dark' horse the Confederates ever saddled. From the start, Pure had an uncontrollable urge to shout him from the rooftops as a champion. So at Salisbury late in May, Lally was only 6–4 when he cantered up in a 16-runner maiden. A fortnight later he had odds of 4–11 laid on him at Lewes. His second easy win encouraged a massive plunge 10 days later, on the first day of Ascot's Royal meeting. After a magnificent-looking colt of Colonel William Hall Walker's, Black Arrow, had won the Coventry Stakes,

Lally was sent off at 5–4 to beat 17 opponents in the Biennial Stakes. He won easily by a length and a half, and was pulled out again next day for the Triennial Stakes. He managed no better than third, but was beaten by only a neck and three-quarters of a length, giving 8lb to the winner and 5lb to the second. In the ruck was a newcomer of the Duke of Westminster's, Troutbeck.

They did things differently in those days. Not content with running Lally on successive days at Ascot, Purefoy – already harbouring classic dreams for the following season – gave his colt a three-week 'rest' and then repeated the dose at Salisbury. First Lally hacked up from two no-hopers, with long odds laid on. The following day he had it all to do in the Champagne Stakes, giving 10lb to Picton, who'd finished half a length in front of Lally at level weights on his Sandown debut. Lally had a hard race to beat Picton narrowly. But just when a modern-day owner and trainer might have decided to bring out the tissue wrapping with the following year's Epsom in mind, Lally was hauled down to Salisbury for the Goodwood train. The Richmond Stakes was the target. It cut up badly, and Lally turned out to have less to do than in a home gallop. Enough now? Not for Purefoy. At the end of August, Lally was sent to Phoenix Park for the £1,500 Phoenix Plate. Besides the rich prize, Pure had an obvious motive in running Lally at the Park. The appearance of the Druid's Lodge wonder horse would add to the prestige (and the gate money) of the racecourse where he and Cunliffe were major shareholders. The race, in which Lally was set to give weight to nine rivals, also provided an opportunity for a real punt. Lally's last three SPs on home territory had been 1–10, Evens, and 1–4. At the Park, enjoying odds against, Pure went for a monumental 'touch.' Lally's main opposition appeared to come from 'Boss' Croker's Athleague, placed in four races at Leopardstown and the Curragh, and receiving 20lb.

Above: Holmer Peard: brilliant vet and judge of a horse, the supremo of Phoenix Park, and judge of the trial gallops (Caroline Wilkinson)

Left: Percy Cunliffe, the master-mind and strategist of the Confederacy; he built Druid's Lodge and its isolated stables (Mark White)

Above: Frank Forester: a noted huntsman and amateur rider, pictured in his capacity as a steward at Bath races (Illustrated London News)

Right: Edward Wigan arriving at Buckingham Palace levee; he was shrewd, silent and devoted to his betting coups' (Henrietta Gaskell)

Above: Jack Fallon, the Confederates' first trainer, overseeing the Druid's Lodge gallops. He was hailed as a genius by *The Sporting Life* (WW Rouch & Co)

Right: Wilfred Purefoy's conservative appearance masked the organiser of some of the biggest gambles in the history of the English Turf (John Bagwell Purefoy)

Above: Percy Cunliffe's new house was close enough to the stable block for him to keep a close eye on the comings and goings. More attention was paid to the comfort of the horses than the lads, who were locked up in the attic every night to prevent stable secrets leaking out (Dare Wigan and *Illustrated London News*)

Left: the Druid's Head inn was closed in the 1890s. Years before, it had incorporated a training yard for the Woolcott brothers (Cyril Henstridge)

Below: Noel Cannon's string walking up the Stonehenge Trail in the 1930s. The open downs made it difficult for touts to spy on the gallops without being spotted (Cyril Henstridge)

DRUID'S LODGE.

RACECOURSE photographers were barely tolerated at the time of the Confederates' heyday. They were discouraged from snapping owners and trainers in the paddock. Hence the public recognised racing personalities from the work of cartoonists. The mysterious Cunliffe and Purefoy were frequent subjects.

MR W. B. PUREFOY AND MR A. P. CUNLIFFE.

Above: Percy Cunliffe drawn by 'The Jabberwock' in *The Winning Post*, 'scouting for touts.' The young woman in the background hints that Cunliffe's interests extended beyond horseflesh

Above right: Cunliffe was a steward at Brighton races. 'The Tout' - Peter Buchanan - drew him with Purefoy on the seafront

Right: Wilfred Purefoy's ski-slope nose made him a cartoonist's dream

Far right: the nose is again prominent in a drawing by the French cartoonist 'Sem' - Georges Goursat

Specially drawn by "The Tout."

MR. W. B. PUREFOY.

"PURE"

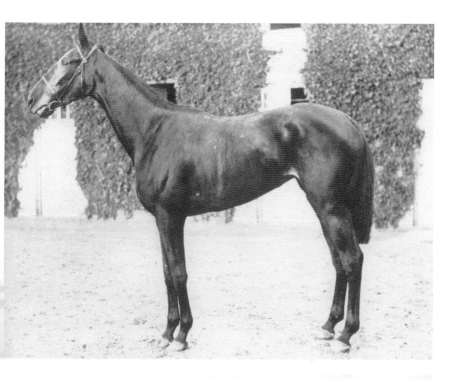

Top: Hackler's Pride, pictured as a three year old after winning her first Cambridgeshire in 1903 (*Illustrated London News*)

Above: As the Cambridgeshire field nears the Bushes on the Rowley Mile, millions in winnings are just three furlongs away. Hackler's Pride leads narrowly before drawing three lengths clear (*Sporting Sketches*)

Right: Bernard Dillon was brought to Druid's Lodge as a boy of 14. His big race wins for the yard included the Cambridgeshire, the Lincoln and the Eclipse. He later married the music hall star Marie Lloyd (*Vanity Fair*)

Above: Jack Fallon in his pomp, in the summer after Hackler's Pride's first Cambridgeshire, pictured with his wife Blanche and their children Nina, John and Margaret. His financial ruin after leaving Druid's Lodge resulted in estrangement from his son (Michael Fallon)

Left: Wilfred Purefoy's Lally, ridden by Bernard Dillon, on his way to the start of the 1906 Derby. The horse's abject performance led to Fallon's departure from Druid's Lodge (WW Rouch & Co)

Ypsilanti winning his second Great Jubilee handicap at Kempton Park, conceding 48 lb to the second horse. Wilfred Purefoy called it, "The only race I ever felt glad to lose money on" (*Sporting Sketches*)

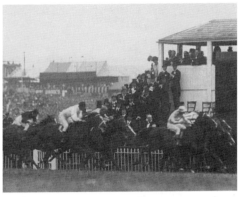

Above: Percy Cunliffe's Aboyeur, winner of the 1913 Derby after a sensational disqualification, and later a victim of the Russian revolution (*Illustrated London News*)

Right: The nail-biting finish of the 1913 Derby. The four horses on the far side are (from the rails) Day Comet, Louvois, Aboyeur and the favourite Craganour (*Press Association*)

Below: The scene at Tattenham Corner after Emily Davison had brought down Anmer and Herbert Jones. The throng behind the running rail would have made it impossible for Davison to 'read' the race and pick out the King's horse (*Press Association*)

Above: Aboyeur's homecoming from Salisbury station. The winner of the Suffragette's Derby looks out, hooded from the stable's horse-drawn Foden box (*Illustrated London News*)

Left: The head-on view of the Derby finish shows how far Aboyeur – with his rider's whip in his left hand – carried Craganour up the Epsom camber. On the inside rail, Day Comet is unnoticed by the judge (J Woodland Fullwood)

Right: Aboyeur's trainer Tommy Lewis, somewhat over-dressed for a beach holiday. He wore an armband in memory of his son and assistant William, who died from burns after an accident at a dance in Salisbury (Hilary Aitchison)

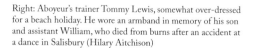

The weight concession was accentuated by bottomless going. Lally was 6–4, Athleague 5–2. Ridden by Dillon, as he'd been for every race since his debut, Lally missed the break, took time to get a run, and joined Athleague at the distance. From the stands he looked the winner, but the journey, the start, the weight and the going took their toll. Shown the whip, he wavered. At the line the verdict against him was a head. Despite his desperately hard race at the Park and the lengthy two-way journey, Lally still hadn't finished for the season. Pure was on a recovery mission – pride as well as punting. For every acquaintance and racing regular who proclaimed Lally as the top two year old of 1905, there was another who wouldn't hear of any but Black Arrow.

Black Arrow was to become the perfect advertisement for those who believe that black horses are ungenuine. But as the morning of Kempton's £1,000, six-furlong Breeder's Foal Plate dawned, he seemed to have just one bit of bad luck to blemish an otherwise tremendous record. On his Newmarket debut in May, Black Arrow had odds laid on him in an 18-runner maiden, winning as all good things should by six lengths. The margin was the same in the Coventry Stakes. Then with 7–100 laid on him at Goodwood, Black Arrow whipped round at the start and took no part. All was well next time in a £1,000 race at Derby, where the odds-layers recovered their nerve sufficiently to bet 1–4 on Black Arrow, against a Lingfield winner of Eustace Loder's called Spearmint.

Giving 3lb, Black Arrow duly beat Spearmint by three lengths. After this race, incredibly, Black Arrow was backed down to as low as 3–1 for the following year's Derby. And so to Kempton. In Lally's saddling box, Jack Fallon heard a voice saying 'Have a look at the best two year old in the world.' Before he could agree, he realised the speaker was pointing at Black Arrow in the next box. 'You won't be saying that after the race,' said Jack sharply. Before the numbers were hoisted into the frame, one foolhardy punter laid £700 to £100 on Black Arrow. In the market proper, odds of 1–4 were asked, with 5–1 freely available against Lally.

It was a miserable afternoon, and shelter was most onlookers' priority, but the canter down was enlivened by an extraordinary sight: Black Arrow's trainer Jack Robinson riding to post after his colt, with a determined expression and a huge dog-whip. Despite – or perhaps because of – the whip, Black Arrow put on a show of prime mulishness. *The Sporting Life* reported him 'all over the place, bucking and jumping and lashing out with his heels.' 'In vain Robinson led him up to the post – round and round he whirled, threatening to play a game of skittles with the others. Meanwhile, Lally was standing as placid as an old sheep.'

During this performance a gamble gathered pace on Lally. At flagfall, Black Arrow had been opposed to 2–5, while Lally was in to 7–2. The start was level, and Dillon sent Lally straight to the front. At the distance Black Arrow closed up behind him, but no sooner had his supporters called him the winner than his tail wind-milled round, and he refused to go through with his effort. Lally ran on strongly, giving 9lb and a length beating to the winner of a £2,000 race at Lewes, Succory, with the disgraced Black Arrow another five lengths in arrears. All of a sudden Lallymania became highly contagious. The epidemic was spread by the win of his Phoenix Park opponent Athleague under 9st in an Ascot nursery, and by extravagant accounts of Lally's superiority on the Druid's Lodge gallops over Edward Wigan's colt Sarcelle.

Sarcelle had made his debut over four furlongs at Windsor in April. He was unquoted in the betting and ran seventh of 11, going on well at the finish. It was a similar story at Newmarket in May, and then Sarcelle landed a tremendous gamble when 'loosed' in the Salisbury Foal Stakes. It was a grand little race for a coup. Five of the seven runners were newcomers – only one of them backed at less than 20–1. There was a fast filly called Sweet Mary, winner of all her six races. And there was Sarcelle, with his two races 'under the arm'.

The Confederates' commission that day was worked by Charlie Mills, a veteran gambler who handled some enormous investments over a period spanning the *multi-million-pound* coup over Winkfield's Pride in the 1896 Cambridgeshire and lucrative assignments for Jack Joel when his filly Jest won the 1913 1,000 Guineas and Oaks. The early betting was 1–4 Sweet Mary and 10–1 Sarcelle. As Mills' commission for Sarcelle circulated, his odds tumbled to 4–1, while the favourite eased to 2–5. Sweet Mary's trainer Jack Robinson was much perturbed – as well he might be – but his filly flew from the starting gate and made the best of her way home. Thanks to her wins, though, she was at a 9lb disadvantage with Sarcelle, and the colt came through to challenge at the distance before wearing her down to win by a neck.

The result had a sensational aftermath. First, at the entrance to the winner's enclosure Ben Dillon was told by the gateman that he hadn't won. He dismounted on the course. The moment Sarcelle was called the winner, Robinson objected. The stewards over-ruled, conceding the 'extraordinary circumstances' of Dillon having been misled. They then initiated a separate enquiry into Sarcelle's sudden improvement. The colt's running was referred to the Jockey Club, where Wigan and Fallon were asked to explain his transformation between Newmarket and Salisbury. Not being 'entirely satisfied with the explanation given,' they told Edward Wigan 'that he must be more careful as to the running of his horses in future.' The explanation, which was justified by subsequent events, was that Sarcelle was as hard a horse to train as any that passed through Fallon's hands. His sire Gallinule was a habitual 'bleeder' and a sire of excitable stock, and Sarcelle proved practically a lunatic. 'To put a saddle on him was to risk your life,' said

Fallon: 'he would take two terrific bounds in the air and unless you happened to be pretty spry you'd be lucky to escape serious damage.'

Before the Salisbury race, Jack persuaded the stewards that it would be useless even trying to saddle him in the paddock. They gave permission for Sarcelle to be saddled alone in a copse, away from the other runners and the noise of the crowd. The result was eminently satisfactory, but at Lewes next time out – with odds laid him on – he gave trouble at the start. Slowly away, he was beaten half a length. Sarcelle then took what was on the face of it a big step up in class, going to Sandown late in July for the season's most valuable two-year-old event, the National Breeders' Produce Stakes.

The 1905 renewal cut up to only eight runners, and bizarrely for what would be a £330,000 race today, Sarcelle's seven rivals had only one win between them. There was one newcomer in the field, an attractive bay filly called Flair, trained at Newmarket by P. P. Gilpin, but she looked backward and was weak in the betting. The paddock pundits watched an exhibition of bad temper from Sarcelle and let him open at 3–1 in the betting. On the way to post, the odds came tumbling down to 6–4. After the tapes rose, Sarcelle was always going well in the leading group. A couple of back-handers from Dillon ensured a very comfortable win. Flair was back in fourth place. The filly, 'when thoroughly fit, will win some nice races,' predicted *The Sporting Life*. On this day, though, the prize-money and the bookies' cheques went to Druid's Lodge.

Sarcelle had three more races as a two year old. Together they confirmed him as one of the best of his generation. First he was sent to Doncaster for a valuable nursery. He received 3lb from Picton – to whom Fallon had a wonderful line through Lally. Sarcelle looked like winning easily as he took the lead at the distance. Weight told, though, and he was beaten half a length by Leopold de Rothschild's Radium, giving 10lb. Picton was back in tenth place.

Sarcelle then won a £1,000 race at Manchester before renewing rivalry with Flair in Kempton's £3,000 Imperial Produce Plate. In the paddock and the ring no one looked beyond Sarcelle and Flair. Sarcelle had given weight-for-sex and several lengths' beating to Flair at Sandown. Now, he was giving 10lb on top of the filly's allowance. And Flair was a fresh horse, while Sarcelle had two recent hard races behind him. In the paddock, Sarcelle kicked and plunged and looked like bolting into the crowd. He got a thrashing from Dillon for his pains. In the race, Sarcelle led to the distance but found nothing when Flair came upside a furlong from the post. Swerving away from Dillon's vigorously applied whip, Sarcelle was two lengths behind Flair at the line.

Wigan had the nice consolation of a seasonal tally of £5,667 from Sarcelle's exertions. Purefoy had even more: the knowledge that on the Druid's Lodge gallops, Lally was consistently and markedly superior to Sarcelle. The rumour machine, fuelled by Purefoy's undisguised infatuation with his colt, soon proclaimed Lally as a reincarnated Pegasus. If he couldn't quite carry Sarcelle and his work rider across Salisbury Plain, it was suggested that he could accomplish practically everything else. All this failed, of course, to take into account the possibility, even likelihood, that Sarcelle wasn't the most reliable of trial companions. Fallon's verdict was that Sarcelle was, 'A mad-headed horse suffering from some mysterious complaint of the brain.'

The stable lads were afraid to go anywhere near the colt, and he would rear up so violently in his stable that Fallon had a net fixed over his head. Yet Purefoy was happy to accept Sarcelle's inferiority on the gallops at face value. Lally, Pure assured his cronies at Romano's, could give 21lb to Sarcelle. This and similar fighting talk sparked a run on Lally for the 1906 Derby that vied for folly with the earlier plunge on Black Arrow. By Christmas, Lally was down to 3–1 – for an event five months away, with 122 entries still standing.

The Winning Post was one voice heard against Lally. Sievier's weekly paper consistently produced forecasts based on form analyses of unsurpassed thoroughness. He acknowledged Lally as 'a smart colt,' but argued that 'The impression he left was that speed rather than stamina will be his forte, and we shall not make him our champion for the Derby.' Significantly, *The Winning Post* team was also adamant in rejecting any consideration of Flair's defeat by Sarcelle: 'That Flair gave her true running must not be supposed for a moment.' The merit of her subsequent win in the Middle Park was closely analysed. The conclusion was that Flair was 'Likely to make considerable improvement, and it will not surprise us if she turns out the best three year old of 1906.' In another review, Sievier cast doubt also on Lally's conformation for the Epsom track. His assessments weren't generally held. The weights for the Free Handicap had Lally top-rated. For Purefoy and the Confederates, the official handicapper's verdict simply set the seal on a great year.

Lally's and Sarcelle's juvenile successes apart, the Confederates' biggest win was with the four year old Queen's Holiday in the Wokingham. The winner of little seven- and four-runner races at Windsor and Worcester as a three year old, Queen's Holiday had cost Forester 4,000 guineas. She started 1905 in unpromising fashion – 25–1 and way out the back in the 10-furlong City and Suburban at Epsom. She then stepped up to a mile-and-a-half to beat a no-hoper less than a length in a match at Gatwick. With this unorthodox preparation for a top sprint handicap, it wasn't surprising that Queen's Holiday went to the races with the lenient burden of 8st 2lb. All Druid's Lodge licked their lips and waited. The Confederates had three runners at the Royal meeting. Lally won on the Tuesday and was third next day. Hackler's Pride won on the Thursday. Come Friday, confidence in Queen's Holiday was sky-high. Dillon had her smartly away. She was six lengths clear after two furlongs, and won pulling up by a length and a half.

The Sporting Life, which had warned its readers to follow any market move for Queen's Holiday, was in ironic form:

> Druid's Lodge may certainly be described as the only
> real rival to Maskelyne and Cooke's House of Mystery [a
> freaks-and-curiosities show in Piccadilly]. It may equally
> well be designated the stable of all the talents, for their
> latest achievement has staggered racing humanity. Rightly
> or wrongly, Queen's Holiday has come to be regarded as a
> filly to show to advantage only over long courses. Stamina
> was thought to be her forte, and she has confounded the
> theoreticians by winning the Wokingham Stakes. In addition,
> she started as hot a favourite as the public could desire, so
> that it was patent that her victory was fully expected. She did
> not open favourite when the betting began but as soon as a
> price was offered 'bar' one, the bookmakers were besieged
> by a crowd of inspired backers, whose numbers grew every
> moment, and all, without exception, wanted to support
> Queen's Holiday. As a manager of a racing stable which bets,
> Mr W. B. Purefoy stands alone.

The newspaper's words must have been salt in an open wound to Pure. The truth was that the nest had been robbed. The Confederates were well and truly pre-empted in the betting.

Fallon had forecast 100–8, but when the Druid's Lodge commissioners slipped into the Ring they were aghast to find that Queen's Holiday had been slashed from a little early 6–1 down to 5–2. It might have been a case of extreme caution by the bookies. They were confronted with an animal that had little chance on form, but every feel of being another Druid's Lodge 'special' – as indeed she was. But Purefoy's agents saw and heard rather more than the usual quiverings of the Ring. Fallon was asked did he know the punters? whom he recalled as 'Lord So-and-So and Mr Isaacstein, nothing better than two wealthy touts of the worst possible type.'

'I've never spoken to them in my life,' swore Jack. Bernard Dillon joined in the protestations of innocence. 'Well, someone has,' said the commission agent: 'they've just taken £5,000 to £2,000 (£187,000 to win £470,000) besides a few other useful bets. What are we going to do?' After a hasty conference, it was decided to make the best of a bad job. Where the interlopers had got their information could only be guessed. Fallon, though, was certain who the offender was – one of his head lads, 'Shadow' Bishiano, nicknamed for his thinness.

'Shadow' was a heavy better in the nightly games of German Banker, and not always a successful one. After a drink or two on the way back from Ascot, Jack picked up his shotgun and chased the lad all round Druid's Lodge. Eventually, 'Shadow' dodged behind a clod-crushing machine. Jack loosed off. He probably only intended to scare 'Shadow,' but he winged him, and 'Shadow' limped ever after.

10.

Lally's Fall and Rise

YEARS AFTER, PUREFOY would recall wistfully that in his three years in training Lally never worked better than in the early spring of his three year old season. Did *The Winning Post* question his stamina? By March Lally was being asked to work a full mile-and-a-half on Ashburton's, giving Sarcelle 14lb and beating him with the greatest ease. For a horse who'd never been entered for the 2,000 Guineas and was aimed solely at Epsom, Lally began his season early and in a quite extraordinary race – a 10-furlong boys' race at Warwick, the last event on a Monday afternoon at the start of April. The race told Pure nothing more than that Lally still had a leg at each corner. With 1–10 betted on, Lally beat a small field, hard held.

Sarcelle's turn came on the Friday of Newmarket's spring meeting. On the Wednesday, the Confederates had watched the 2,000 Guineas with the closest interest. A whole raft of Derby fancies were entered, and their performances could hardly have been more encouraging for Wigan and Purefoy. The runners finished in a heap – a head and a neck between the first three. The winner, Gorgos, had finished in the ruck behind Lally at Ascot the previous June. The once more hyped Black Arrow ran another deplorable, sulky race.

Two days later, Sarcelle faced two more Derby fancies – Picton and Radium – over the last 12 furlongs of the Cesarewitch course. Sarcelle was a good thing to beat Radium. He was 10lb better off for the half-length beating at Doncaster – in which race Picton had been in the next parish. But excusing that as Picton's only bad run in 1905, there was little between him and Sarcelle on other lines of form. They betted 10–11 Picton, 13–8 Sarcelle, 10–1 Radium. Picton, amateur-ridden at a pound overweight, went down to Sarcelle by a head, with Radium half a length back in third. Confidence in Lally's Derby chance redoubled.

In the 1,000 Guineas, the red-hot favourite was Sir Daniel Cooper's Flair, conqueror of Sarcelle at Kempton the previous October. Ridden by Ben Dillon, Flair won – as *The Winning Post* had long predicted – by an easy three lengths. P. P. Gilpin immediately nominated the Derby as her target, but how could that worry Druid's Lodge? A simple calculation based on home gallops with Sarcelle put Lally a mile in front of Flair.

Purefoy had his worries, though. It was vexatious that Lally had never been entered for the 2,000 Guineas; he must have won it easily. Now, he had to decide whether or not to give Lally one more 'prep' before Epsom. Another win would have made the colt even more valuable, though in truth the price on his head wasn't Pure's main concern. By bragging of Lally's prowess during his two year old career he'd invited frequent offers. If they were only half as large as reported, they were a King's ransom. Now, as the Derby approached, Sir Ernest Cassell's agent tabled an offer of £15,000 – plus a £10,000 contingency (£2,345,000 in total) if Lally proved successful at Epsom. It was a distraction Pure didn't need, the more so as Fallon and Peard were starting to wear anxious expressions.

Lally was entered in mid-May for a valuable 10-furlong stakes race at Newmarket. Peard advised Purefoy against running. For no obvious reason, the Derby favourite began walking rather feelingly after his Warwick race. Peard couldn't find anything wrong, but he suggested that if there was a doubt over the colt's legs, and not much racing in them, then better the Derby than a prep race. After a long consultation with Fallon, Pure made his decision: to Newmarket. It looked like pot-hunting. The race cut up to four runners – Lally, the 2,000 Guineas winner Gorgos, an enormous colt called Malua who seemed held on previous running with Sarcelle, and a 33–1 outsider. The race was as unsatisfactory a trial as could be imagined. Lally was heavily bandaged in the parade. Malua was kicked at the post by Gorgos. The Guineas winner made the running to the Bushes, where Lally drew to the front. Down into the Dip he looked likely to win unextended, but in a moment the roars of acclamation changed to 'The favourite's beat!' as Lally fell in a heap. Dillon applied the whip, and in a driving finish Lally held on by a short head and a head from Malua and Gorgos.

The result created a sensation. Lally's detractors said he would have been third, not first, if Malua hadn't been kicked and Gorgos hadn't swerved in the last few yards. One critic insisted that Lally was touched in his wind. *The Winning Post* declared that coming out of the Dip, 'His lack of stamina began to assert itself,' confirmed by the 'Special Commissioner' of *The Sporting Life,* who dismissed Lally as 'Obviously a non-stayer'.

The plainest judgement came at the call-overs. The word was out that P. P. Gilpin's 1,000 Guineas heroine Flair had broken down on the gallops, and before the Newmarket Stakes Lally was backed again at 6–4 and 11–8 for Epsom. Picton and Malua were 7–1, Gorgos 100–8. After the race, Lally was pushed out to 9–4, Malua was in to 6–1, and a bet of £4,500 to £200 was noted about a second string of Gilpin's, Spearmint.

The bet was part of a £47,500 commission worked by one of the first and greatest Pressroom punters, the Newmarket-based Archie Falcon. Born in poverty in Yorkshire, Falcon made a living out of journalism and a fortune out of betting. On occasion he placed bets for Purefoy, but in May 1906 he had a hunch that would send an icy blast across Salisbury Plain. The hunch began with a tip from a lad at Gilpin's Clarehaven stable that – never mind the 1,000 Guineas winner Flair – the Gilpin Derby horse was a real dark 'un: Spearmint.

While Lally was catching trains all over the place as a two year old, Spearmint (by the Melbourne Cup winner Carbine, out of Maid of the Mint) had just three runs. He was all out on his debut at Lingfield to beat Succory by a head and 4lb; he was slammed by a best-behaviour Black Arrow; and then he ran unplaced under top-weight in a Newmarket nursery. On his last two outings he was ridden by Bernard Dillon, and it was Dillon who kept popping up at Clarehaven to ride work on Spearmint. It was work that Archie Falcon went to great lengths to observe.

Three times in the fortnight before the Derby, Spearmint worked with the triple classic-winning Pretty Polly and the Cesarewitch winner Hammerkop. Spearmint shaped 'wonderfully well' in the first gallop. He matched Pretty Polly in the second, receiving 6 lb more than weight for age. Then a week before Epsom, over the full Derby distance, he came out the great filly's superior. It was said 'Mr Gilpin hoodwinked the Newmarket touts' - apart from Archie Falcon. Bernard Dillon lied to the *Sportsman* that, 'So far as I know, Spearmint has never been tried with Pretty Polly' – having himself ridden in the trials. He knew that Lally was not, after all, the good thing that the Confederates had supposed.

The fortnight between the Newmarket Stakes and the Derby was, Fallon confessed, 'one of the most trying times I have ever undergone.' He, the brilliant horse master and Holmer Peard the brilliant vet went over Lally's legs twice a day. And twice a day they couldn't find anything wrong. Yet the colt was moving more and more gingerly in his work. His evident unsoundness wasn't helped by a spell of abnormally dry weather, and consequent bone-hard gallops. Even Purefoy was forced to admit that Lally was going shorter and shorter, but still he clung to the hope that Lally had time and distance in the Derby to warm to his work and reproduce the best of his two year old form.

In his final serious bit of work on the Saturday before the Derby, Lally spread a plate badly. Pure's consternation was so great that he refused to allow anyone in the yard to touch the twisted shoe. The Royal farrier Bob Todd was summoned. He fitted Lally with a special plate and boot that appeared to relieve all trace of lameness. The sighs of relief could be heard all the way from Druid's Lodge to the London bookmakers.

Rumours that all wasn't well with the horse were rife. The knock-out that began after his unconvincing win in the Newmarket Stakes had continued. On the eve of the big race, Lally – once a 5–4 shot – was out to as long as 13–2. Spearmint had meanwhile been backed from 20–1 to 7–2. His owner Eustace Loder made no secret of his convictions. He told the racing journalist Harding Cox 'You had better have a bet on mine. If I'm not mistaken he will win, and easily.' Archie Falcon too had given his readers one word, consistently and emphatically: Spearmint.

Purefoy left Jermyn Street at four o' clock on the morning of Derby day to motor down to Epsom and watch Lally canter on the course. He was delighted with what he saw. Lally moved well, and Pure's somewhat dented confidence was boosted sky-high again. His restaurant Romano's had long been booked for a post-race victory celebration. The money was already down as never before, but the odds on offer on Derby morning were simply too tempting to leave unpunished. As he'd done a hundred times, Purefoy reassured himself with the form book.

The talking horse Spearmint? Lally was 6lb superior on a line through Succory, a stone better through (the admittedly unreliable) Black Arrow. Malua and Gorgos? Lally beat them at Newmarket, didn't he? Leopold de Rothschild's Radium or Mr Dugdale's Picton? Could their supporters be serious, Pure wondered? Hadn't Radium only narrowly beaten Wigan's Sarcelle in receipt of 10lb – with Picton behind; and hadn't Lally himself given 10lb to Picton and beaten him fair and square in the Champagne Stakes? Every way that Pure looked at it, his colt had the form beating of every horse ranged against him at Epsom. Most of them, indeed, by such a margin that Sarcelle came into the reckoning as a distinct place possibility.

On and off the racecourse all day long, the Druid's Lodge commission agents piled into Lally. By the time the Derby runners came out onto the course, he'd re-emerged as clear favourite at 3–1, while Spearmint retreated to 6–1. Sarcelle was 25–1. When the better judges watched the parade, many of the doubts about Lally re-surfaced. He seemed very light – over-trained, some said. When the horses turned to canter back past the stands, several moved noticeably short on the hard ground: none worse than Lally. In the last moments before the off, he was pushed out again to 4–1.

Purefoy and the Confederates knew their fate almost as the tapes rose. Lally jinked sharply to his left and lost several lengths. Dillon seemed to panic, and made up the lost ground too quickly on the uphill back stretch, dashing Lally up among the leaders after a couple of furlongs. It was clear that he hated the ground, running with his head high and jaw cocked. As the outsider Troutbeck (far behind Lally at Ascot the previous summer) made the running at a strong pace, Lally dropped back as quickly as he'd rushed up. He came down the hill to Tattenham Corner sideways. A long way from home,

Dillon had given up. Afterwards, Ben said the colt wouldn't take hold of his bit – that he'd never known him in such a mood.

Meanwhile, Troutbeck led into the straight, only to be headed by Picton. Cruising up behind them came Danny Maher on Spearmint. He took on Picton at the distance, and with a peep over each shoulder nudged Spearmint home by a length and a half. Two lengths back came Troutbeck, with Radium fourth. Spearmint lopped over two seconds off the Derby record – a sure indication of the firmness of the going. Far back came Sarcelle and Lally in fourteenth and fifteenth place. Purefoy – the poker-faced, iron-nerved Pure – wept publicly at the unsaddling. A friend said later that it wasn't the fortune lost in bets, or the knowledge that all his friends would be facing similar horrendous settlements the following Monday. It was simply that Purefoy loved Lally obsessively, and couldn't bear the humiliation of his downfall.

The dinner at Romano's was cancelled. The other consequences were equally swift. A furious post-mortem at Druid's Lodge challenged Dillon's and Fallon's roles. There was a suspicion that after Dillon's work-riding at Clarehaven, he and Fallon had both backed Spearmint, if only to hedge their bets on Lally. Purefoy believed that Dillon had been got at by the bookmakers – hence the slow start and the stamina-sapping attempt to recover the lost ground too quickly. Grudgingly, the evidence of all eyes – that Lally hadn't handled the course, the ground or the trip – was accepted. Dillon was more or less exonerated. Purefoy's fury fell on Fallon. If he hadn't actually done anything to stop Lally, he'd certainly been negligent in over-training him, asserted Pure. The atmosphere worsened when *The Winning Post* arrived with a cruel cartoon of a disconsolate Purefoy peering through his binoculars, captioned *Lally – Still Looking for a Buyer*.

Whether Fallon was fired or resigned is a moot point. Thanks to Hackler's Pride and the 280 or so winners he'd trained and backed at

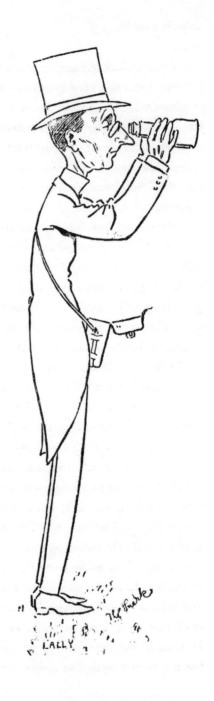

'Still Looking for
a Buyer' cartoon by
'The Snark' published
in *The Winning Post*,
2 June 1906

Druid's Lodge, Jack was a rich man. He was a founder shareholder at Newbury racecourse. He had £68,000 in the bank – a little north of £6 million today. He invested his savings in two farms and a training yard – Scotland Lodge – at Winterbourne Stoke, a couple of miles north of Druid's Lodge. Off he went in a spanking new Panhard limousine. Fallon had a tremendous reputation after his ten years with the Confederates, and he was quickly patronised by several prominent owners.

Jack's place at Druid's Lodge was taken, as *The Sporting Life* had predicted, by his fellow Irishman Tom Lewis. Tommy came from County Down, and was for some years assistant to Gisbourne Gordon at Brownstone Lodge on the Curragh. Together they won pretty well every major race in Ireland, notably with the horses of Mr Fulton. When Fulton decided to bring his string to England he brought Lewis over too. The first fruit of that partnership was a big gamble with Comedy in the 1891 Cambridgeshire. After Fulton's death, Lewis set himself up in a small way as a public trainer at Netheravon, going along quietly with a yard of a dozen or so horses. His obvious attributes so far as Cunliffe and Purefoy were concerned were maturity (he was 56), knowledge of training on Salisbury Plain, and a pedigree that included a successful coup in a big handicap.

Lewis's first, nerve-racking task was to retrieve something for Lally from the disaster at Epsom. It was a tacit admission of stamina failings that his next race should be over the straight six furlongs at Hurst Park. He was up against a small and poor field, and he never came off the bridle in giving a newcomer, Crusader, 15lb and a three lengths beating. For his next outing, Lally was back in the first division – Ascot's St James's Palace Stakes. Here he faced three who'd finished in front of him in the Derby: Beppo (sixth), Plum Tree (ninth) and Black Arrow (tenth). Back to a mile, Lally was a hot favourite to beat them. Black Arrow was the outsider of the quartet, but every dog has his day and to general disbelief Black Arrow decided this was it. Dillon got first run with Lally and looked like winning easily, but along came Black Arrow like the most honest animal in the world to beat him a length, with Beppo in third. After the race Lally's bridle broke. He got loose and galloped free about the Heath, luckily without coming to any harm.

Lally's next race was the Eclipse. Some regular rivals were in the line-up – Beppo, and the 2,000 Guineas winner Gorgos. By now, confidence in Purefoy's wonder horse was on the wane. A strong Press lobby proclaimed it was now obvious that he didn't stay a yard beyond a mile. For the first time in 15 races since his two year old debut, Lally didn't start favourite. He again moved horribly on the way to post, drifted in the betting, sweated up badly and ran deplorably, making no show at any stage.

1906 had one more nasty shock for Purefoy. Lewis found a valuable seven-furlong race at Gatwick in October that seemed tailor-made for Lally to end the season on a high note. The Surrey Stakes had a first prize equivalent to £181,000, and only six runners. Lally was odds on. He led to three furlongs out and was then headed and beaten readily by Crusader, whom he'd himself beaten easily in June. He didn't even hold second place. There were roars of derision from the Ring. 'There is no greater curse to an owner than the possession of a good horse who will not race,' sympathised *The Sporting Life:* 'Such unfortunately is Lally, who refused to do his best in the Surrey Stakes.'

Another *Life* correspondent wrote: 'That Lally was a good horse as a two year old is a proposition very few would dispute. He was a good horse in the spring. But whatever he may have been a few months ago, he is now distinctly moderate.' Every similar opinion, and there were plenty like it, was further gall to Wilfred Purefoy. He still believed his horse was a champion, but he had to recognise the truth of the

Irish adage: 'No foot, no horse.' Lally was sent back to Tipperary and turned out to grow new feet in the paddocks at Greenfields. At Druid's Lodge, a private farrier, Bert Ford, was recruited to minimise foot problems in the future.

Lally came back into training the following spring, and confirmed the growing prejudice against him by finishing unplaced in a seven-runner apprentice plate in May. He was backward, though, and *Racing Up To Date* advised subscribers to 'ignore the race completely.' In another boys' race soon after, Lally scrambled home by a head from three bad opponents. He was 7–4 against, where a year before he might've been 1–20. Who could have imagined they were watching the leading prize-winner-to-be of 1907? As the bookmakers would discover, Purefoy had spent the winter baiting a mighty trap. It was sprung in the Hunt Cup. The sackcloth and ashes surrounding the Derby, not to mention subsequent disappointments, had lulled the handicapper into inattention. Lally not only got into the Hunt Cup with just 8st, but old friends like Malua and Succory were weighted worse with him than when he'd beaten them the previous season.

When the first prices were published for the Ascot handicap, Lally was 33–1 and 25–1. Purefoy and those of his friends who hadn't given up hope had every chance of recovering losses. On just one day, a week before the race, Lally was backed to win £5,000 (£461,000). Although Lally moved notably well to post, the continued desire of the Ring to show its contempt for him meant that he started at the generous odds of 100–6. That didn't stop him winning the Hunt Cup as you'd expect a former Derby favourite carrying 8st to win it – easily. Drawn in mid-field, he tracked the group racing up the far side of Ascot's straight mile until his lightweight New Zealand jockey Leslie Hewitt sent him on two furlongs out. He went quickly clear, ears pricked, and was eased close home to win cleverly by half a length from the 1905 winner of the race, Andover.

Three days later *The Winning Post* had two comments on Lally's win. The first was Sievier's own: 'Lally [is] the best managed horse we can ever call to mind. We readily admit that his performances deceived us, and from a Druid's Lodge point of view, Mr W. B. Purefoy is to be highly congratulated. [At Wolverhampton] he just scrambled home a head in front of a mediocre animal like Guy Middleton [who] could not have won the Hunt Cup with 5st on his back.'

The paper's Newmarket correspondent spat blood:

> The handicappers have been hoodwinked into weighting
> Lally on a couple of miserable efforts in apprentice plates
> when unfit and not fancied very much. After this lesson they
> surely should require no manifesto from the Stewards of
> the Jockey Club to open their eyes to the wiles of the man
> who engineers the affairs at Druid's Lodge. Our trainers at
> Newmarket have few opportunities of bringing off coups of
> this description, their horses being subject to acute criticism
> of a goodly number of horse-watchers every time they do
> work, and if there is a screw loose of any kind it is known to
> everyone through the medium of one or other of the sporting
> papers. The handicappers, therefore, ought to err on the side of
> leniency to those horses of whom they know everything, and
> be judiciously careful of those who are under the care of the
> men who have so often made their work look ridiculous.

After Ascot, Lally was beaten at Windsor when sprawling left and then right in the closing stages of a 10-furlong handicap, going down by three lengths to a very moderate rival. His critics bounced back. They said he sulked and that he conclusively showed that he didn't stay 10 furlongs, even on an easy course like Windsor. Surely, then, it was nothing more than vainglory that persuaded Purefoy to take Lally to Sandown in mid-July for another try in the mile-and-a-quarter Eclipse? Stamina doubts apart, there was a formidable opponent, Sancy. After finishing in front of Lally in the Derby, Sancy had much the better subsequent form. As a three year old, he went on to win the Prince of Wales Stakes and the Zetland Stakes. His 1907 campaign was a dead-heat for the Chester Vase, followed by a five-length win at Ascot from the Jubilee winner Polar Start. Sievier's preview of the Eclipse was short and to the point: 'Comment on the race would be superfluous, Sancy standing out as one of the biggest certainties there ever was in racing.'

That kind of talk has a way of inviting Nemesis to come calling. For the first time in over a year, Purefoy was beating the Lally drum openly and insistently. His friends were told to back Lally, without any reservations or qualifications. At Druid's Lodge, Pure and Lewis and Dillon made their tactical preparations. Pre-race, Lally had sometimes shown temperament. Lewis would ask permission from the stewards for Lally to miss the parade and walk across the course alone to the start. In the race itself, Dillon would try to switch Lally off for as long as possible. With no apparent chance of outstaying Sancy, he would delay his challenge to the last moment possible.

On a boiling hot afternoon at Sandown, Sancy was a predictably warm favourite at 2–5. Lally was a firm 5–1 second best. The presumed best of the three year olds, the Derby fourth Bezonian, was the only other backed among the seven runners. In the paddock, Lally looked at peak fitness. With the stewards' assent, he missed the parade and was led down quietly. Soon after the start, Otto Madden sent Sancy into the lead – but at a dawdle. Along the railway straight Lally was anchored plumb last, and the Ring, assuming this was a 'bye' day, shouted extended odds. Round the turn, going easily in the lead, Madden took a pull at Sancy, slowing the pace still further. Behind him, Dillon slipped Lally through into third. As they came in line for home, Bezonian threw down his challenge to Sancy. Madden, who still hadn't moved, could see Bezonian under maximum pressure – but hidden from him on Bezonian's other side was Dillon.

For a few strides, Ben gathered Lally; then with a furlong to go he sat down and rode for all he was worth. Alive at last to the danger, Madden picked up his whip and Sancy responded. But now Lally was level, and answering every call from Dillon. In the last half-furlong the two colts were neck and neck. The crowd roared them home, and in the final few yards Ben hit Lally for the first and only time in the race. He and Lally, Madden and Sancy went by the post together.

There was pandemonium in the stands and in the Ring. Many expected to see a dead-heat signalled. But after a tense few moments, up went the number Purefoy was praying for – 1. The distance was the shortest of short heads. Congratulations were showered on Pure from all sides. Those who'd been appalled and embarrassed to see him weeping at Epsom were now almost as surprised to see him laughing and grinning from ear to ear. Well might he grin. 'They say Mr Purefoy won a great parcel,' wrote the Press. Most probably. What was certain was that he collected a mammoth £9,785 (£903,000) for owning and nominating the Eclipse winner. Better still, Pure was vindicated. His home-bred prince had come at last to claim his kingdom. Lally had stayed 10 furlongs, run home like the gamest horse in training, and won the most valuable race in England.

The pundits divided equally between those who lauded Dillon and those who damned Madden. 'The verdict is Dillon eclipsed Madden,' punned *The Winning Post*, and Sievier's verdict was harsh in the extreme.

Most certainly Madden should take a voyage round the world. We should recommend a sailing ship. He has not been married long, and it is not too late to look upon this proposal in the light of an extended honeymoon. A worse performance than his riding of Sancy in the Eclipse Stakes we have never witnessed. For a jockey with a reputation his exhibition was execrable, and had it been an apprentice's maiden effort [it] could not have been worse.

Others took the more charitable view that Dillon had ridden a blinder. For all too short a time, Dillon was a jockey of the highest class. After his distant view of Spearmint in the 1906 Derby he rode that horse to victory at Longchamp in the Grand Prix de Paris. Remembering Pretty Polly, P. P. Gilpin took no chances. A special steamer was hired to take Spearmint across the Channel. Dillon took no risks, either. Foreign big-race winners were distinctly unpopular in Paris in those days. Hearing that the French jockeys were planning a rough ride for him, Bernard led throughout, quickening the pace whenever a challenger (or attacker) drew up to him. He and Spearmint had just enough in reserve to win, all out, by a neck. Pretty Polly notwithstanding, Gilpin was to nominate Spearmint as the best horse he ever trained.

The praise showered on Dillon for the brilliant ride he gave Spearmint was nothing compared to his canonisation after Lally's Eclipse. *The Sporting Life* headlined it *Dillon's Triumph*.

You may praise the horse, and you may praise the trainer. When all is said, however, it must be allowed that Bernard Dillon was the hero of yesterday's contest for the Eclipse Stakes. He has ridden good races before – many of them; but never has he distinguished himself to quite the same extent as he did on this occasion.

Here we have before us an example of jockeyship that is absolutely beyond criticism. No horseman breathing could

have done more than Dillon did, nor have done it better. I am
not writing in this strain simply because Lally defeated Sancy.
If the verdict had been the other way round I should still have
been justified in expressing the opinions I am now offering. It
would have been the simplest thing in the world to have got
Lally beaten, but Dillon was doing the right thing all the time.

Lally's career ended with anti-climax, running for no obvious reason
in a £500 handicap at Doncaster, and finishing second trying to give
away 35lb. Purefoy sent him to Newmarket sales at the beginning of
December, where he was withdrawn after the bidding reached 8,000
guineas. There was some question as to whether he was seriously for
sale. One cynic said that if there really was a genuine bid of that
size for Lally – and if it was refused – 'then there were *two* fools at
Newmarket.'

Lally went back to Greenfields in triumph. With £11,555 in win
money, he comfortably headed the list of winning horses in 1907.
Almost alone he was responsible for Purefoy's fifth place in the list
of winning owners. The chestnut had several years at Greenfields,
but despite having the most desirable mares put to him, he never got
a really good horse. In 1915 he was quietly sold to stud in Italy. He
headed the list of winning sires there in 1922, but was destroyed that
August. His stock were non-stayers.

11.

Classic Near-misses

TWO YEARS ON from the Press forecasts that changes and cutbacks were imminent at Druid's Lodge, both had come to pass. Jack Fallon had gone. Lally's disastrous failure in the 1906 Derby hastened his departure, but he would have moved on in any case. As to cutbacks, there'd been a wholesale pruning of costs during the winter of 1905–6. No longer were invalids kept on the payroll in the hope that Jack could patch them up for a minor touch in a bad selling race. The result was that after tallies of 37 and 39 winners in 1904 and 1905, the Druid's Lodge score sheet plummeted to just 15 wins and £6,671 (£290,000) in prize money in 1906.

In 1907, with Tommy Lewis installed and Lally at the head of the prize-money list, the Confederates bounced back to 24 winners and £20,553 in win and place money. Flushed also with the proceeds of huge coups over Lally's Hunt Cup and Eclipse, Purefoy asked Holmer Peard to look out for some likely yearlings in Ireland. Forester in particular was keen to leave behind the stable's 'hot' reputation. Press sneers and Lord Durham's thinly veiled attack on Druid's Lodge co-existed uneasily with his Establishment role as Master of the Quorn.

At the sales at the end of 1907, the Confederates spent £6,125 (£565,000) on a dozen or so purchases, the most costly being a £2,100 yearling at Tattersalls, a colt by the 1895 2,000 Guineas winner St Frusquin out of Spearmint's dam, Maid of the Mint. Holmer Peard had meanwhile negotiated to buy eight yearlings from the Tully, Kildare stud of Colonel William Hall Walker. The agreed price was £10,000. The St Frusquin colt, who was called Mat-o-the-Mint, ran in Forester's colours and turned out to be useless. But the Tully purchase was one of the better bloodstock buys: most of the eight won races. They included Charles O'Malley, taken by Percy Cunliffe, and Edward Wigan's Ulster King, winner of four races and over £5,100 in prize money.

It was Charles O'Malley who led the Confederates' search for classic glory to add to their collection of major handicaps. He was a magnificent son of the 1897 Coventry Stakes winner Desmond, out of Goody Two Shoes, a mare by the Triple Crown winner Isinglass. Goody Two Shoes was one-eyed after a collision with a post in a race at the Curragh. As the result she was a danger to other mares and foals, and had a paddock to herself with Charles O'Malley. He was described by a visitor to Tully as 'a great long larruping colt foal with splendid back and loins.' 'Great' proved an understatement: Charles O'Malley required an extraordinary amount of work to get him fit. He also worked lazily. The Druid's Lodge set-up wasn't sympathetic to malingerers, whether real or imagined, so Charles found himself accoutred with hood and spurs. He had a particular loathing of spurs. The resulting trial of wills on the gallops gave the big bay colt an undeserved reputation for temperament and ungenerous work. In the circumstances, it was a tribute to all concerned – most particularly the horse – that he should emerge as one of the top two year olds of 1909. He was palpably backward on his Epsom debut, and ran outpaced and unplaced. He was well fancied six weeks later for the

Windsor Castle stakes, and won from 16 rivals in a finish of necks and heads and half-lengths.

Charles O'Malley then went to Newcastle for the Seaton Delaval, where he was again a narrow winner after a slow start and trouble in running. On his first attempt at six furlongs he won the Richmond Stakes at Goodwood in a canter, giving weight all round. Purefoy reckoned that 2–5 would be a fair price, but a furore in the Ring over one of Leopold de Rothschild's meant the Druids enjoyed plenty of Evens. Charles O'Malley went pot-hunting up to Manchester in mid-September, odds on and giving weight to second-raters in the valuable Autumn Breeders Foal Plate; and ended the season when again odds on in the Prendergast Stakes at Newmarket, where he failed by a length to catch a fast-starting American-bred. Victory in the Windsor Castle, Richmond and Seaton Delaval Stakes gave Charles O'Malley realistic prospects of a say in the following year's big races. As it turned out, he had his say, but his place in turf history has more to do with his jockey than his own achievements, useful though they were.

Bernard Dillon was by now gone from Druid's Lodge. He had a handsome retainer from P. P. Gilpin, plenty of good spare rides, and was sharing a house in Newmarket with Leslie Hewitt and the American jockey Lucien Lyne. Not for the first time, Purefoy went talent scouting. Pure's record was already outstanding: he'd found and imported the unknown Fallon and the teenaged Dillon. Now, he made his greatest contribution to racing posterity: he convinced Steve Donoghue that his future was in England.

Donoghue was to win his place in that select quartet of flat-race jockeys who stand supreme on the English turf – Fred Archer, Steve himself, Sir Gordon Richards and Lester Piggott. Unlike the others, Steve was a late starter. Having fled his indentures at Newmarket, he rode his first winner in the French provinces at 21, and his first winner in Ireland at the Phoenix Park in April 1907. Success in England didn't come until May 1909, when Steve was already 25. By contrast, Archer rode his first winner at 13, Richards at 17, Piggott at 12. Donoghue's hard apprenticeship in France reaped its reward in Ireland. He was a curious transplant, born in Warrington, with a sackful of winners round the tough little tracks of the French provinces. The Irish weighing room couldn't be expected to welcome this colourful intruder, and it didn't, though Steve gave as good as he got round the Irish country courses.

By 1909, he was so far the best of his generation in Ireland that he won the jockey's championship despite missing the last month of the season after illness. Purefoy and Peard had spotted Donoghue's talent quickly, though it's possible that at first they considered him only as a lightweight; he went to scale then at little more than 6st. During 1909 Purefoy several times asked Steve to ride for Druid's Lodge, and offered him a retainer. Donoghue turned the offer down, believing that his commitments to his retaining stable of Phillie Behan would make the travelling to and fro impossible. On his way to Greenfields that October, Pure ran into Donoghue at the Kingsbridge station in Dublin. Once more, he asked Steve – could he cross to England? Frank Forester expected a winner or two at Newmarket next day. For the first time, Donoghue agreed, and composed a wire to Tommy Lewis. No sooner had it been sent than he collapsed; two days later he was operated on for a ruptured hernia.

Having held onto his lead in the Irish jockey's title race despite a long convalescence, it must have been plain by now to Steve that his future lay back home in England. There was more racing and better prize-money. The start of the flat in 1910 saw him unwell again, having contracted a fever when watching coursing's Waterloo Cup with friends. He was unable to accept an offer from Purefoy to ride Christmas Daisy in the Lincoln. His absence made no difference –

Christmas Daisy was well beaten – but Pure continued to press Steve to accept a retainer. 'I didn't feel up to taking on the responsibility of all the riding for such an important stable as Druid's Lodge was then, as I still often felt far from fit,' said Donoghue, but recalled in his memoirs that 'I was constantly crossing to England to ride, principally for the patrons of that stable, and I seemed to be very lucky when riding for them.'

Purefoy wanted Donoghue's services so badly that Steve was invited to stay at Druid's Lodge – 'An invitation that was very seldom accorded to a jockey,' as he pointed out. During his stay he partnered Charles O'Malley for the first time. The colt's preparation for the classics had gone badly. The 2,000 Guineas was bypassed because he had a cough. None the less, as the Derby approached he worked a stone better than the Confederates' other Epsom hope, Wigan's Ulster King. As he got up on Charles O'Malley, Donoghue was told, 'He doesn't do much. Get hold of that stick and wake him up a bit.' He ignored the instructions, and the colt went kindly enough for him, so Cunliffe asked him to take the mount in a last-minute prep for the Derby – an 11-furlong race at Windsor on the Saturday, just four days before Epsom.

At Windsor, Charles O'Malley had only two opponents for a modest prize. One was a no-hoper, the other the potentially useful Willonyx, set to concede Charles O'Malley 7lb. Charles was blinkered and spurred, and Cunliffe as before urged Steve not to spare the whip if some 'waking up' was needed. It wasn't. Despite looking so backward in the parade ring that 'If a safety razor had been attached to his stomach he would have made an excellent lawnmower,' as one onlooker joked, Charles O'Malley made all and won in a common canter. Donoghue had no recourse to whip or spurs. The result created a stir in the Derby betting. Donoghue had indirectly answered Cunliffe's question after Windsor – 'Would you give him any chance in the Derby?' – by agreeing to take the ride. The Confederates got out their trials books, confirmed the evidence of the gallops – and backed Edward Wigan's Ulster King.

Until his Windsor race, Charles O'Malley had appeared at a cautious 100–8 and 10–1 in the Derby lists, despite his non-appearance on the racecourse and gossip about his set-back. Ulster King stood at 25–1 and more. The opportunity suddenly presented itself for a tremendous sting. The news broke that the French champion jockey George Stern had been booked for Ulster King. Then on the Monday and Tuesday before the Derby, Druid's Lodge 'faces' made persistent enquiries about Wigan's horse at the call-overs. Simultaneously, reports circulated that Ulster King had left Charles O'Malley for dead on the Druid's Lodge gallops. Perhaps Percy Cunliffe hadn't yet realised that Steve Donoghue was an enthusiastic punter; even so, he put him away in tremendous style by letting it slip that Ulster King had won a trial by a distance, with Charles O'Malley tailed off last. The sensitive nerves of the Derby betting were well summed up by *The Winning Post*:

> The inmates of Druid's Lodge so far have bolted and barred themselves within its four walls, and the man in the street who assumes he knows anything about this stable and its prospects for the Derby is guessing. No stable can have better trying tackle, and if a decided move is made in favour of either of the two Irishmen, and it is maintained, Druid's Lodge should be followed with the avidity of a savage.

When the move was made, it was contrived, but it had the desired effect. Ulster King dropped from among the outsiders to 100–8 on the day of the Derby. Charles O'Malley, partnered by a lightweight who had a reputation in Ireland but was unknown in England, drifted friendless out to 33–1. The Confederates weren't confident. They couldn't be, with the likes of the 2,000 Guineas first and second Neil Gow and Lemberg in the field, and with their horse having had an interrupted preparation. But they were hopeful. Purefoy deployed a hidden – positively subterranean – each-way commission on Charles O'Malley.

Steve Donoghue was unaware of this as he walked Epsom on Derby morning. It was his first Derby ride. He couldn't imagine that he was to ride the winners of six Derbys and eight other classics. He was a debutant, and nervous. None the less, he gave Charles O'Malley a copybook ride, never out of the first half-dozen. He was carried a little wide down the descent to Tattenham Corner, but immediately closed to the rails in the straight. He ran on stoutly into third behind the Ben Dillon-partnered favourite, Lemberg, with the 2,000 Guineas winner Neil Gow fourth and Edward Wigan's slow-starting Ulster King running on in sixth. Lemberg broke Spearmint's record for the race.

If there was a hard luck story it was Neil Gow, who sprang a curb in the last few days before the race, but overall it was a Derby that went entirely to form. It was a good Derby, too. Neil Gow and Lemberg ran a pulsating dead-heat in the Eclipse. Ulster King was to collect a huge consolation prize – £3,457 – in the Princess of Wales Stakes at Newmarket in July. There were some big days in store for Charles O'Malley too. He landed some nice place bets for the Confederates by his third place. Their elaborate knock-out was the subject of some sarcastic comment in *The Winning Post*.

Why the excellent services of Stern, France's premier jockey, should have been wasted by his being put up on what was the inferior of the stable is one of the many enigmas for which Druid's Lodge has become disagreeably notorious. For [Ulster

King] to be supported by the public at 100–8 on the day of the
race, and Charles O'Malley to go out to 33–1, it is obvious that
the patrons of Druid's Lodge are not seeking election to the
Jockey Club.

As usual, opinions of this sort were water off a duck's back to Cunliffe.
Having got Charles O'Malley fit, he wasted no time in taking his
colt to Royal Ascot a fortnight later for the Gold Vase. He won the
£1,100 prize comfortably, and then joined Lemberg in a raid on the
Grand Prix de Paris.

The Grand Prix then occupied the position that the Prix de
l'Arc de Triomphe enjoys today – immense prestige to the winner,
a huge prize, and an opportunity for the English *turfistes* to amuse
themselves in Paris for the weekend. English cash made Lemberg
a red-hot favourite in the main enclosure, the *pesage* – 6–4 to win,
odds on to place – though the shrewder punters made their way
down the course to the *pelouse*, where they could have over 7–1 to
win, 2–1 to place. Charles O'Malley was 10–1 in the *pesage*, 17–1 in the
outer enclosures. The third English hope, James Rothschild's Derby
absentee Bronzino, was a derisory 1,183–1 and 317–1 to place.

The invaders faced a formidable home team, led by the top French
two year olds of 1909, Nuage and Reinhart, each become high-class
three year olds, Nuage winning the Prix de Guiche and Prix Greffulhe,
Reinhart running second in the Prix de Saint Cloud. They also faced
highly testing conditions. It rained all weekend, up to and during the
Grand Prix. The ability of both Lemberg and Charles O'Malley to
stay the mile and seven furlongs in what had become a swamp was
uncertain. Danny Maher advised Lemberg's connections not to run.
Purefoy made no secret of his anxiety for Charles O'Malley.

Steve Donoghue, who had more experience of riding in France
than any English-based jockey, made an uncharacteristic blunder

in the early part of the race. Charles O'Malley missed the break, whereupon Steve – with 15 furlongs to make up his ground – shot Cunliffe's colt right through the 17-runner field in the first half mile. What Steve later defended as 'Every sort of bad luck in the race', included being badly struck into, with a back tendon cut. By the time the field reached the windmill where the Arc now starts, Donoghue had bustled Charles O'Malley into the lead. Up the hill and *après le petit bois,* Charles still led, with Nuage on his heels, followed by Danny Maher sitting quiet as a mouse on Lemberg, Bronzino close up. Donoghue still led down the descent to the straight, where Maher brought Lemberg up to challenge. In line for home, Charles O'Malley plugged on up the rails, with Lemberg apparently cruising alongside him. Nuage, Bronzino and Reinhart – running on from way back – were in line abreast close behind. Just as every English visitor called the Derby hero the winner, Maher sat down to ride his finish and found nothing. Nuage slipped through between the tiring English pair and quickly went clear. Reinhart was a decisive second. Bronzino, Charles O'Malley and Lemberg finished in a heap, in that order.

About the only happy Englishman in Paris that day was Jimmy Rothschild, who collected the equivalent of £700,000 for the *pari-mutuel* place odds in his 'pony each way' bet on Bronzino with his London bookmaker. For Cunliffe, the Grand Prix was the culmination of a cruelly unlucky season with Charles O'Malley. In finishing alongside Lemberg in Paris, his colt showed that with a trouble-free preparation he would have gone close to winning at Epsom. In the Grand Prix, he must have been no worse than second with a more judicious ride and without injury. Worst of all, with the St Leger appearing a lay-down for Charles O'Malley, his tendon put him out for the season after just four races. He continued to be dogged by bad luck the following year. After two prep races, he went to Ascot strongly fancied for the Gold Cup. He was second favourite behind Willonyx, who'd made tremendous progress since being run over by Charles O'Malley at Windsor the year before.

Cunliffe had left nothing to chance. Tommy Lewis not only had fitted Charles O'Malley with blinkers and spurs; the colt's ears were stuffed with cotton wool for good measure. Not surprisingly, he was on his toes in the paddock, and so reluctant to go onto the course that a farrier led him out. At the start, he threw his head up, catching Steve Donoghue in the face and knocking him out of the saddle. Donoghue was evidently dazed, but he remounted, and in the race Charles O'Malley went down to Willonyx by a neck in a thrilling finish.

Donoghue blamed everything on the new bridle that Charles O'Malley wore that day.

> I took particular care not to touch the horse with the spurs. My orders were to wait with him, and these I found impossible to carry out, owing to the new reins slipping through my fingers every time I tried to take a pull at the horse. The whole trouble was caused, and the horse lost the race, through the use of the wretched new bridle. All irritated as he was by the maddening feel of the cotton wool in his ears, he kept boring at me as I tried to hold him back, and away the tiresome new reins would go slipping, till my fingers were all cut and bleeding, and after reaching the mile-and-a-half post I simply had to let the horse stride along, which however seemed to suit him better. Half-way up the straight Willonyx passed me, went on, and looked like winning by two or three lengths. Directly Charles saw the other horse in front, he put in a most determined challenge, and went after Willonyx with giant strides, overhauling him rapidly, and at the finish he was

only beaten by a neck. I am positive Charles O'Malley would
have won the Gold Cup, in spite of all the other drawbacks,
but for that new bridle!

If this reads strangely defensively it is because Steve was hardly in a
fit state to do the horse justice. Concussed when Charles O'Malley
butted him at the start, he surprised spectators by riding into the
unsaddling enclosure and asking them, 'When do we start?'

As a five year old Charles O'Malley won just an amateurs' event
at Alexandra Park. Once it became apparent that he'd had enough
of training, Cunliffe sent him to Purefoy's stud at Greenfields. Not
surprisingly, for a colt who could easily have been the winner of a
Derby, a Grand Prix and a Gold Cup – and if there was any justice
would have won at least one of the three – he proved popular. He
had a full book of mares at once, with plenty of breeders turned away
disappointed. Purefoy doubled his fee from £49 to £99 after the 1914
covering season, but he still filled for 1915. He took a year or two to
justify the confidence, but he sired the 1918 Cambridgeshire winner
Zinovia, then the Percy Cunliffe-owned Charlebelle, winner of the
1920 Oaks. Suggesting that he was mainly an influence on the bottom
half of a pedigree, he also sired Malva, dam of the 1930 Derby winner
Blenheim and of King Salmon, second in the 1932 2,000 Guineas
and Derby, and winner of the 1933 Eclipse.

It was after Charlebelle's Oaks – reinforced by the success of
another Charles O'Malley filly in 1920, the unbeaten two year old
Pharmacie, that Purefoy decided to go banco. He and Holmer
Peard put together a syndicate of Irish breeders who paid Percy
Cunliffe £40,000 for Charles O'Malley. Like so much associated
with the horse's racing career, the investment was a disaster. Little
more than a year later, right at the start of the 1922 covering season,
Charles O'Malley broke a leg at Greenfields and had to be destroyed.

Ironically, one of his sons, Light Dragoon, won the Cesarewitch for Frank Forester that autumn.

Many worse horses than Charles O'Malley have won a classic. That was small consolation to the Confederates, for whom he was one of four frustrating placed runners in the classics in quick succession. Frank Forester's filly Bracelet (bred at Greenfields by Collar out of a 200 guineas mare, Isis Belle) won the Cheveley Park as a juvenile and ran second in the 1909 1,000 Guineas. Then came Charles O'Malley's third in the Derby in 1910.

That season, Druid's Lodge had two home-breds of Frank Forester's with some promise. One was Royal Tender, a bay colt by Persimmon out of Tender and True. Royal Tender won Salisbury's Champagne Stakes as a two year old, and ran up a hat-trick the following spring at Newbury, Kempton and Kempton again before the Derby. He was third at Epsom to Sunstar and Stedfast, beaten two lengths and four. He then ran second in the Gold Vase before a fatal accident on the Druid's Lodge gallops. Another horse kicked out and Royal Tender's leg was shattered.

The Derby meeting of 1911 was particularly frustrating for Forester. After Royal Tender's third, Druid's Lodge had high hopes of Tootles in the Oaks. She was a daughter of his own prolific winner Lady Drake, by John O'Gaunt. As a two year old, Tootles won just a 17-runner nursery at Nottingham under Steve Donoghue, but she had several good placings to her name, including a second in the Cheveley Park.

Tootles began 1911 with a minor win at Bath, and she was then the subject of a sustained gamble all the way down to 7–2 favourite for the Oaks. But from out of the clouds dropped a rank outsider, Cherimoya, who flew past Tootles to win going away by three lengths. Forester was entitled to feel robbed. The winner had never run before, and never ran again. With her out of the way Tootles – five lengths in front of the third filly – would have been an easy winner herself. She proved expensive to follow after Epsom, with further seconds in the Nassau Stakes, the Park Hill and the Sandown Foal Stakes.

Tootles stayed in training for another two seasons, but eventually suffered the fate common to horses who aren't quite of the highest class, carrying punitive weights in the top handicaps and invariably finding a lightweight or two to beat her. She was second in the 1912 Cesarewitch to Warlingham, conceding 21lb – a result over which Bob Sievier won so much that he distributed around £1,000 in ready-money gifts on the racecourse.

Druid's Lodge's near-misses in 1909, 1910 and 1911 gave the lie to the sneers that the Confederates had no interest in the classics, only in manipulating handicaps. Enthusiastic breeders like Purefoy and Forester wanted nothing more than the prestige of a classic winner for their studs. And as they showed with Tootles, it's as possible to work a major commission in a classic as in a handicap. Maybe more so, since as Purefoy complained, it was harder than ever to get the money on, so obsessive was the bookies' attention to Druid's Lodge. 'If I want £50 on a race now, I sometimes have difficulty in getting on. A friendly bookmaker lays me the odds to a 'pony' and then pushes me in the chest and jumps down and backs the animal himself with another bookmaker.' Pure had his ways and means, though, and the stable was still to be mightily feared in a handicap. As it showed with an Irish gelding of Holmer Peard's: Christmas Daisy.

12.

The Daisy's Double

'ABOUT 3 PM yesterday a solitary horseman might have been seen wending his way across the Heath. This was Christmas Daisy winning the Cambridgeshire.' Few horse races have been described as exactly, in as few words, as the 1909 Cambridgeshire by the racing reporter of *The Tatler*.

The bay gelding Christmas Daisy had an odd pedigree. He was by Vitez, a stallion standing at the Ballykisteen Stud of George Edwardes, out of Daisy, a mare who was sold for 15 guineas. Daisy was a shy breeder, but her first foal, Eremon, won the 1907 Grand National. Her third, Christmas Daisy, won two Cambridgeshires. Bred by James Cleary at Cashel in Tipperary, Christmas Daisy was passed to Holmer Peard. By the end of his two year old season, the Daisy had repaid none of Peard's expenses, running four times and placed just once. It was a good placing, though, third at Leopardstown to 'Boss' Croker's 1,000 Guineas winner Rhodora.

In his races, Christmas Daisy marred his chances by starting slowly. Come the spring of 1908, he again missed the break in maiden events at the Phoenix Park, so that on his third outing at the Park he had an attendant at the start to lead him in. The lad's presence seemed to have the opposite effect to that intended. Christmas Daisy got off even more slowly than usual. The *Irish Field* said that Christmas Daisy's chance 'Was seriously prejudiced by the man who was leading him at the starting gate holding on too long.' The private handicapper Charles Richardson went further and suggested that the action was deliberate. Holmer Peard, always alive to the smallest slur attached either to his horses or to Phoenix Park, let alone both, sued Richardson for libel.

This fine donnybrook was set into sharp focus a fortnight later when Christmas Daisy carried 6st 9lb in the valuable Commemoration Plate handicap at the Curragh. Steve Donoghue rode and fancied the top-weight in the race, and told how:

> We were at the tapes all ready for the start when I noticed, drawn next to me, a neat-looking bay that had a familiar look about it. There was a small jockey perched on him, sitting still as a mouse, with his eyes fixed straight ahead, breathlessly watching for the tapes to go up. 'I say, isn't that Christmas Daisy?' I asked the lad. No reply. 'Hey you, *is that* Christmas Daisy?' Still no reply. And with that we were off, and away went Christmas Daisy, the first out of the gate. He showed us a clean pair of heels all the way, and won in a canter.

There's a suggestion of hindsight here. Donoghue had no special reason in June 1908 to pay close attention to a lightly weighted gelding that he'd never sat on. After riding him to win a Cambridgeshire, perhaps Christmas Daisy's early days became rather clearer. None the less, Steve's account strongly suggests a coup – and coup there was. The *Irish Field* said that Holmer Peard had backed Christmas Daisy 'to win quite a substantial stake' at the returned odds of 7–1.

The handicapper Richardson's opinion having been to some extent justified by Christmas Daisy's win, nothing more was heard of Peard's libel action.

There was a lot more heard of the horse. At the Phoenix Park in May 1909 he was overhauled and beaten into second place over 10 furlongs – having held a clear lead for over a mile – which set Peard to thinking about a tilt at the Hunt Cup. Christmas Daisy was shipped to Druid's Lodge. There, he was tried against the best tackle the stable could provide, and went well enough for the Confederates to speculate each-way for the big Ascot handicap. Then Tommy Lewis was approached by a neighbouring trainer, Francis Cobb, with a request for galloping companions for his own Hunt Cup hope, Dark Ronald. Naturally enough, Lewis set up exactly the same trial as for Christmas Daisy. To his surprise, Dark Ronald made an even better show than Peard's gelding had done. The Confederates were in the happy position of hedging their bets over Christmas Daisy by backing Dark Ronald, who started favourite at Ascot. For seven furlongs in the Hunt Cup, Christmas Daisy was giving as good as he got in a head-to-head with Dark Ronald, but at the distance his rival confirmed the evidence of the Druid's Lodge gallops by coming away quite comfortably. Christmas Daisy was run out of second place close home.

Dark Ronald was a pretty good horse. He landed a £100,000 punt in the Hunt Cup for his owner, the colourful South African goldfield millionaire Sir Abe Bailey. Dark Ronald himself was sold for £25,000 to a successful stud career in Germany. Christmas Daisy also changed hands. Holmer Peard told Forester before Ascot that he had a more than useful tool. Did Forester want to take him for £1,500? Forester declined. He told Peard that he had as many horses in training as he wanted, and that Mastership of the Quorn was draining even his considerable resources. The upshot was that Christmas Daisy became the property of a typical Confederacy syndicate. Percy Cunliffe and Edward Wigan (in whose colours he ran) took majority shares, Purefoy had a leg, and Peard kept a contingency in the event of success in the Hunt Cup.

After his excellent third at Ascot, Christmas Daisy was a close-up fourth in the valuable London Cup at Alexandra Park. Then no sooner were the weights published for the Cambridgeshire, and Christmas Daisy there for all the world to see with 6st 6lb, than he bolted up from 20 rivals in the £1,000 one-mile Peveril of the Peak Plate at Derby. The 'Special Commissioner' of *The Sporting Life* hailed the ready-made Cambridgeshire winner.

> The Cambridgeshire, as usual, contains a high-class entry, but
> it seems a pity that the work of the handicapping committee
> should have been apparently marred within a few hours of its
> publication by the spread-eagling performance of the four-
> year-old Christmas Daisy at Derby, let off with 6st 6lb in the
> nine furlongs race of the Newmarket Houghton meeting.
> Yesterday he ran away with the Peveril of the Peak Plate from
> a field which included some smart sprinters, none of whom
> could ever get on terms with him, and he won as if another
> stone would have made no difference.
>
> Of course, he has a penalty, but even so the extra 10lb leaves
> him a serious bugbear to owners of others, seeing that his
> weight is now but 7st 2lb. Surely this Irish-bred horse ran well
> enough in the Royal Hunt Cup at Ascot to make handicappers
> chary of how they dealt with him, even granting he was soon
> afterwards beaten into fourth place for the London Cup at
> Alexandra Park – which was not bad form either, but one
> cannot compare a straightaway dash to that helter-skelter
> contest which has been described as once round the frying-pan

and finish down the handle. In such a race things may easily
happen to prevent a horse showing his best form.

Still, there it is, and one wishes the trio of handicappers
well out of what appears, at first blush, an awkward situation.
There are others, of course, but Christmas Daisy displayed
such a burst of speed yesterday, which is so essential for a
Cambridgeshire, that he must be bad to beat if he keeps well.

With the wounds of Hackler's Pride still raw, the Ring rapidly
advanced Christmas Daisy to 10–1 favourite, eight weeks in advance
of the Newmarket race. Plenty of speculators with no more to go on
but the association of Druid's Lodge and the Cambridgeshire dug
deep for the Daisy. What should happen but that Christmas Daisy
went to Manchester for the £2,000 Prince Edward handicap. He was
9–4 favourite, penalised for his win at Derby, but still receiving 2lb
from the second favourite Succour, a good handicapper (winner of
the Chesterfield Cup and third in the Jubilee) but no world-beater.
Christmas Daisy led at the distance, but was quickly overhauled
by Succour, and beaten two lengths. At once, a strong prejudice set
against him for Newmarket. Hadn't he been an obvious trier and still
beaten? And wasn't there a line through Succour to a colt of Robert
Sherwood's called Land League, which gave Land League plenty in
hand of Christmas Daisy?

From early October through to the day of the race, Christmas
Daisy was remarkable for moving very little in the betting. He was
100–7 on 6 October, and the same price three weeks later when the
race was run. Like many another horse, though, Christmas Daisy
didn't know his odds. He didn't know that the Confederates thought
he lacked the class for the race, especially under his penalty. He
certainly didn't know that Land League – sure to beat him on the
book – had been got at in his stable before the race. Land League

was found with a clean cut four inches long and two inches deep in his chest. Yard security had been tight, so the maiming was almost certainly the work of a stable employee. Suspicion fell on a lad who left the yard soon after, but despite a careful search no weapon was found. Months later when some ivy was being cleared from a wall in the yard a rusted razor blade was discovered. Land League missed the Cambridgeshire, and though he was back in training the following year he never recovered his form. There was never the slightest suggestion that Druid's Lodge was behind the nobbling of Land League. Owner-breeders like Forester, Peard and Purefoy cared too much for horses to stoop so low.

Land League's absence left Lord Carnarvon's three year old Mustapha the favourite for the Cambridgeshire to beat 18 rivals. His trainer Matt Dawson thought him a certainty. The jockey Charles Trigg was promised a £1,000 bonus if he won. He did his best, but on ground as soft as was ever seen at Newmarket, neither Mustapha nor the five others preferred to Christmas Daisy in the betting had the remotest chance with Edward Wigan's horse. His lightweight jockey Charlie Ringstead had Christmas Daisy away like a flash. He was six lengths clear after two furlongs. Mustapha was given every chance, always in the front of the pursuing group. He took a clear second place at the Bushes, stimulating an enormous cheer from his supporters. But Christmas Daisy, with the only unmuddied colours in the field, never faltered for a stride. He came up the hill five lengths in front of Mustapha, with another three lengths to the third horse.

The result was greeted with enthusiasm among those who'd joined the rush for Christmas Daisy after his win at Derby, by gloom down at Whatcombe where fingers were badly burnt over Mustapha, and by consternation at Druid's Lodge. One punter, wreathed in smiles, told Edward Wigan how he had £50 on Christmas Daisy. He'd enjoyed a nice win, and he hoped Wigan had done the same.

'You had £50 more on him than I did,' was the sour reply. It would have been only human nature for Wigan to harbour a suspicion that his co-owners had in some way stitched him up. His wife Edith disapproved strongly of what she saw as Cunliffe's moral laxity with the young ladies, and no doubt she encouraged Wigan's irritation.

The first outward sign of disharmony at Druid's Lodge since Jack Fallon's departure was the appearance of Christmas Daisy in the Newmarket December sales catalogue, 'To dissolve a partnership'. The Daisy was knocked down for £2,500 – to Percy Cunliffe. Before long, peace broke out between Wigan and the others. For his final season in training, Christmas Daisy again wore Wigan's colours. He was somewhat backed for the 1910 Lincoln – the stable commission was only £600 – but disappointed. He then finished eighth in the City and Suburban at Epsom in April, miles behind his Newmarket victim Mustapha, at level weights.

After his run at Epsom, Christmas Daisy disappeared from sight, so far as the English flat season was concerned. When the Cambridgeshire weights were published, the horse had been absent for over four months. He had no immediate prep race entries. What to make of it? One answer was that Christmas Daisy had been kept on the move in France – hurdling. Another was that unlike the previous year, a commission was already working its way through the London clubs. After a few small bets at the end of September, £1,000 to £60 was laid on 9 October, £4,000 to £320 the following day, £1,000 to £90 twice the day after. With Christmas Daisy already backed to win over £635,000 and down to 10–1, there was a two-week lull, during which the bookmakers cautiously pushed him out to 100–6 in the face of strong support for one or two others, among them Whatcombe's Mustapha.

The race looked difficult for Mustapha. The handicapper, after a year or two's respite from Druid's Lodge, had taken a decidedly generous view of Christmas Daisy. Perm any of three possibilities: the 1909 Cambridgeshire result was a total fluke; or the 1909 Cambridgeshire result showed that Christmas Daisy went in the mud and nothing else did; or the 1910 City and Suburban result truly reflected the respective abilities of Mustapha and Christmas Daisy. The outcome was that Mustapha, thrashed at Newmarket in 1909, was 1lb worse off with Christmas Daisy in 1910. The evening before the race, 100–6 was offered against 'the Daisy' in the Subscription Rooms. Those odds and £1,000 to £80 were taken. The next morning, a tremendous gamble was loosed by Purefoy: every fraction from 100–8 down to 7–1 was taken, and few at Newmarket managed to bet at the returned odds.

Steve Donoghue was in the saddle, in place of Ringstead a year earlier. Otherwise, nothing changed. The Daisy bounced out under the tapes and set a fast clip for home. At the Bushes, Steve had a long look round at the toiling favourite Whisk Broom and the running-on Mustapha, and actually took a pull at Christmas Daisy. As a year before, Whatcombe's supporters had their hopes raised by Mustapha closing momentarily, but the moment Donoghue met the final incline he sent Christmas Daisy away to win comfortably by a length and a half. The feat of sending out the same horse to win successive Cambridgeshires had never been achieved until Hackler's Pride's wins in 1903 and 1904. Now, Druid's Lodge had repeated it with Christmas Daisy. And to emphasise the dominance of the gambling stables, Whatcombe supplied the runner-up in three of Druid's Lodge's four Cambridgeshires.

There was plenty of Press criticism for the lenient treatment of Christmas Daisy by the handicapper. *The Sporting Life* commented:

Precisely why the winner was so favourably handicapped against his victim of last year is not easily understood.

Christmas Daisy has not been out since April, and surely
it was a risky proceeding on the part of the handicapper to
estimate him solely on his Lincoln and Epsom running, and
to totally disregard his extraordinary performance last year.

Wryly, the *Life* reporter confessed to having left the horse out of his
calculations:

Although the establishment of which Christmas Daisy is an
inmate cannot be described as a popular institution from the
ordinary backer's point of view, it is impossible to withhold
a word of praise for the cleverness with which its racing
business is conducted. Its secrets are rarely if ever allowed
to leak out. Mistakes are rarely made, though it is on record
that last year Christmas Daisy did to some extent surprise his
connections.

In far more poetic vein was Bob Sievier in *The Winning Post:*

In centuries to come when Druid's Lodge stands on lonely
Salisbury Plain a ruin, a sister to its neighbour Stonehenge,
which has ever been a mass of mystery, it will doubtless be
pointed out as an historic monument in connection with the
story of the Turf. The guide, as he takes tourists over the spot
in an aeroplane, will point out Stonehenge as mysterious, and
the ruins of Druid's Lodge as more mysterious still. Doubtless,
he will add that it was a famous place, not a philanthropic
institution, but once known as Druid's Lodge. But what
further explanation may be offered and what adjectives
brought into play in describing those ruins is a matter too
far ahead for us to conjecture. One thing the Salisbury Plain

showman may megaphone to his load in the sky, namely,
that 'Christmas Daisy won the Cambridgeshire twice in
succession, ladies and gentlemen, the second time so easily
that Mr Cunliffe might have ridden it himself.'

Though notching another place in racing's record-books with
Christmas Daisy was satisfying to the Confederates, of far greater
importance was that they landed another fabulous gamble. Arthur
Hamblin had backed the Daisy to win close to £1 *million* for them,
and Pure had another five or six agents working parallel commissions.
The most visible confirmation of the coup came when Cunliffe spent
some of his winnings on hiring a professional golfer from Scotland
to design and construct a nine-hole course either side of the road
below Druid's Lodge. The professional was a kindly soul who tried
to teach the lads to play golf; not at all what Cunliffe intended.
When they started breaking down the edges of the bunkers with
their bicycles they were banned from the place altogether, except for
caddying, and for holding up traffic when play crossed the road. Not
to be outdone, Edward Wigan had a nine-hole course built in the
park at Conholt.

After the Cambridgeshire, Christmas Daisy was sent to Percy
Cunliffe's trainer at Chantilly, Morley, to be prepared for a big
hurdle race at Nice. The raid was unsuccessful, as was an attempt
the following spring at the French Champion Hurdle at Auteuil.
Watching the Auteuil race, Frank Forester noticed that Christmas
Daisy jumped rather big for hurdles. 'The Daisy' was brought back to
England to be trained for the 1911 Lincoln, but he showed signs of
unsoundness. Cunliffe and Wigan retired him immediately, and gave
him to Frank Forester, who if he had accepted Peard's first option
on the horse would have been the owner of four Cambridgeshire
winners in seven years.

Forester took Christmas Daisy to the Quorn, where he said 'He developed into a perfect hunter in no time, for he had a beautiful mouth in a double bridle.' Christmas Daisy and Forester had half-a-dozen happy years together in the hunting field. After a busy day early in 1918 Forester's groom called to ask whether he'd noticed anything wrong with the horse, as he hadn't lain down? The vet diagnosed a cracked pelvis, and Christmas Daisy was rested until the autumn. Forester got up on him, but before they'd gone a couple of miles, slowly, the old horse stopped. He was put down in his own stable and sent to the kennels.

13.

The Suffragette's Derby

ABOYEUR WAS A savage, notorious even at a time when evil-tempered horses were far more common than nowadays. George Lambton provided a memorable description of the hazards they presented in *Men and Horses I Have Known:*

> Nearly every stable would contain one or two really savage horses, and when as occasionally happened one of these got loose, there would be a regular stampede to get off the Heath.
>
> I remember on one occasion when I was the only person left on the Limekilns, and it happened in this way: it was at the time that I was suffering from my back and could not ride. I was on foot waiting for my horses to come up the gallop when I heard a most extraordinary noise proceeding from the plantation that runs along the side of the Bury road. Then a loose horse dashed out from the trees, and stood there roaring and trumpeting in a way that I have never heard before or since.
>
> I at once recognised that it was a noted savage called Prince Simon, owned by the French sportsman Monsieur

Lebaudy and trained by Golding. My assistant, Harry Sharpe, was with me and I hurried him off to turn my string on to the Waterhall ground out of the way of this mad brute, who would savage anything he came near. Away went Sharpe, and everyone else made themselves scarce. I could see and hear Prince Simon charging about the plantation in a mad state of fury kicking and biting at the trees. He then went for Golding, who rode a white pony. Golding discreetly left his hack. It was said that he climbed up a tree.

The pony galloped off towards Moulton, pursued by Prince Simon, and I thought all was well. But somehow the pony eluded his pursuer, and the Prince again appeared on the Limekilns. Standing there, lord of all he surveyed, he was a fine sight, although rather too close to be pleasant. Still, I did not think he would bother about me upon foot, but, finding nothing else worth his attention, he suddenly came charging down at me. It was not a pleasant position, as I was more or less of a cripple. I had my shooting stick with me, and when he came at me I gave him a crack over the head which made him stand on his hind legs and roar with rage.

At this moment, by the greatest piece of luck, Golding's white hack emerged from the trees on his way home. Prince Simon, catching sight of him, went after him like a dog after a rabbit, and chased him home to his stables, where they managed to let the pony into a box and shut the door on his pursuer. They were not able to catch the savage till late in the afternoon.

Mercifully, stable staff, riders and racegoers don't often encounter risks of that kind today, partly because savages are actively discouraged by the authorities. The talented but wayward sprint handicapper

Ubedizzy was warned off after trying to eat his lad in the paddock at Newmarket in 1978. More especially, stable routine is much more sympathetic now. Druid's Lodge wasn't alone in sweating its horses rugged up in saunas, or in the endless pummelling with whisks, which were a regular part of conditioning a horse. Spurs were commonplace. Colts were fitted with horrible wire and spiked contraptions to prevent them masturbating. Not surprisingly, conditions of this sort produced a fair number of moody horses. Some of the measures taken to make them more amenable only made them worse. Jack Fallon, exasperated by a rogue who had maximum potential and minimum enthusiasm, put him to pulling a heavy plough for hours on end.

The easiest course with a trouble-maker was to off-load. George Lambton had a colt he called 'a regular savage but a real good horse'. This was Chiselhampton, a 500 guineas buy who won the Sandown Foal Stakes as a two year old and four valuable handicaps the following year, but he had a fearful thrashing on the gallops from Fred Rickaby, and some gruelling races. A season and a half went by without further success, while Chiselhampton became unmanageable. He not only used to bite the turf; he even tore at his own chest. Purefoy's faith in Fallon's ability to tame practically anything on four legs led him to pay 155 guineas for this monster at the December sales. For once, Jack had to admit defeat: 'Among the many welshers I've had through my hands, I must award the palm to Chiselhampton.' None of the Druid's Lodge lads would go anywhere near the horse. As a parting shot, he badly mauled the groom sent from Tattersalls to collect him for the sales. An intrepid and overweight trainer from Lewes paid 18 guineas for Chiselhampton to send him hurdling. Word soon came back that his new trainer had lost a lump of his stomach to Chiselhampton. Percy Cunliffe laughed his head off. 'What's he complaining about? What's one mouthful with all he's got?' was the extent of his sympathy.

Aboyeur was as nasty an equine character as one could wish to avoid. He was almost black, by Desmond out of Pawky, a maiden mare who was by the Hunt Cup and Gold Cup winner Morion, himself an evil-tempered animal. The wonder was that he wasn't gelded at a very early stage. However great the temptation, it turned out well for Percy Cunliffe that it was resisted. He was Aboyeur's fourth owner. The colt was bred by T. K. Laidlaw, sold as a colt to James Daly, and passed on to Holmer Peard, who sold him to Cunliffe and Wigan for 1,000 guineas. Aboyeur recouped £517 of that outlay as a two year old with a second at Sandown and just one win, the Champagne Stakes at Salisbury in July. It wasn't a strongly contested race, but it was a major surprise that he ran, let alone won. The previous day he unshipped his work rider on the road outside Druid's Lodge and went on a solo six-mile gallop all the way into Salisbury. Eventually he was caught in Fisherton Street in the town centre, and stabled overnight at Wilton House.

There were any number of two year olds who boasted better form than Aboyeur when the prospects for the following year's classics were discussed at the end of 1912. *The Winning Post* and others nominated Bower Ismay's Desmond colt Craganour as the likely winner of the 1913 Derby. Craganour was a reject before he went into training, sold with his dam Veneration II by his breeder Eustace Loder to Sir Tatton Sykes's Sledmere Stud for £1,700. Craganour was sent by Sykes to the yearling sales at Doncaster, and made top price of 3,200 guineas. Despite signs of temperament, he won five of six races as a two year old for Bower Ismay and his trainer Jack Robinson, including the Middle Park and Doncaster's Champagne Stakes. Craganour and Aboyeur, the two sons of Desmond – himself no more than a precocious sprinter – were separated by no less than 21lb in the Free Handicap. Purefoy, though, thought that behind the poor form and the flashing teeth there was improvement in

Aboyeur. With the example of Charles O'Malley – another son of Desmond – fresh in the mind, Pure was also convinced that Aboyeur would turn out to be a stayer. The result was that all winter when Percy Cunliffe had a pound or two in change, he backed Aboyeur for the 1913 Derby.

The races that the two colts ran before the Derby seemed to confirm the yawning gap between their abilities. Aboyeur was unquoted in the betting and finished a poor fourth in the Easter Stakes at Kempton Park on the opening day of the season. Craganour, after a prep race when backward, went to Newmarket and 'won' the 2,000 Guineas. 'Won' has to be qualified because, having passed the post a length or more to the good over Louvois and Meeting House, Craganour was placed second. The horses finished wide apart, with Craganour under the rail where the judge Charles Robinson was standing. Apart from the well-established optical illusion that favours the far side, Robinson had of course no photograph to fall back on.

The trainer of Louvois, Dawson Waugh, saw his colt's number upmost in the frame and remarked, 'They've made a bloomer. They'll damn soon take it down.' Craganour's jockey William Saxby swore that he'd won by a clear length-and-a-half. A storm of criticism descended on Robinson. A story circulated in Newmarket that after giving Louvois's number to the boardman as the winner, Robinson called the number of Meeting House as second. At that point Robinson's assistant interrupted him and asked where did he place Craganour? Robinson replied that he hadn't seen Craganour's colours in the finish. He was told that if Craganour hadn't won 'he was certainly very close up.' Whereupon Robinson directed that Craganour's number be put into the frame after that of Louvois, followed by Meeting House in third. Whatever the merits of this account, Robinson defended himself vigorously. 'They are saying that Saxby won. What they should say is that he ought to have won.'

The view formed that Craganour had been going so well that Saxby should have ridden him home, especially in a classic, by a margin beyond any judge's scope for error. Saxby was replaced by Danny Maher in Craganour's next race, the 10-furlong Newmarket Stakes. Craganour was opposed by his 2,000 Guineas 'conqueror' Louvois and by Jack Joel's Sun Yat. He beat Sun Yat easily by a couple of lengths, with Louvois a further length-and-a-half behind. Those who held that Craganour had been robbed in the Guineas felt vindicated. The bets that had made Bower Ismay's colt the winter favourite for the Derby were reinforced by a public gamble that brought him down to 6–4 favourite for the race. If there were any doubts at all about him, they concerned his jockey. Danny Maher had won on him at Newmarket, but Danny's retaining owner, Lord Rosebery, had a runner in the Derby: Prue.

Prue was a no-hoper. Rosebery, who formed a devoted, almost father-and-son relationship with Maher, invited him to get off Prue to take the ride on Craganour. With extraordinary, some would say misguided, loyalty, Maher insisted on honouring his retainer. Jack Robinson might have said bygones were bygones and invited Saxby to reunite with Craganour. Saxby had after all ridden Craganour to all his wins as a two-year-old, as well as in the controversial 2,000 Guineas. Against Saxby, though, was an unpleasant suspicion that he might have divided loyalties. His indentures as an apprentice had been held by Eustace Loder – and between Loder and Bower Ismay there was bad blood amounting to hatred.

'Lucky' Loder was a soldier, a bachelor with little interest other than his horses. He was a steward of the Jockey Club. In his eyes, Bower Ismay was a parvenu, a tradesman (the Ismays were shipowners). Worse, Ismay had for some time conducted a semi-public affair with Loder's sister-in-law. There seemed very little Loder could do to make his displeasure felt by Ismay, but plenty that Ismay could contrive to embarrass and enrage Loder. He went to top price at the sales to buy what the breeding world knew was a Loder 'cull,' Craganour. He got Loder's protégé Saxby to ride him and to rub in Craganour's emergence as the best two year old of 1912.

When the judge at Newmarket called Louvois the winner of the Guineas, Loder was the senior presiding steward. Many were surprised that the stewards didn't call an enquiry into the judge's verdict. Surprise turned to paranoia among Craganour's connections. Had Saxby secretly agreed with his mentor Loder to win – if he was in a position to win – by a small enough margin that the judge could call the result against Ismay's colt? The suspicions were absurd, but the upshot was that Jack Robinson spurned Saxby, who knew Craganour so well, and sent to France for Johnny Reiff.

It was a bizarre choice. Memories of the American dopers were still fresh and bitter among the turf's Establishment. And in the weighing room, the home jockeys had become increasingly angry at owners' and trainers' habit of calling for cross-Channel talent for fancied mounts in the big races. 'Rivalry between the English riders and the men borrowed from France is becoming a serious problem,' noted 'The Scout' in the *Daily Express*. In his *History of the Derby Stakes*, Roger Mortimer described the 1913 renewal as, 'The most sensational, the most tragic and the most unsatisfactory in the history of the race.' The verdict is accurate in every respect.

Fate sent a rich and varied cast to Epsom that first Wednesday in June. Among the jockeys were the aggrieved Saxby, the ruthless Johnny Reiff, the equally ruthless Epsom rider Frank Wootton, the celebrated Danny Maher and Steve Donoghue, and the obscure Edwin Piper. In the senior steward's place was the austere Eustace Loder, hoping with every fibre that Craganour wouldn't win. In the judge's box, Robinson again. In the owners' enclosure, Percy Cunliffe and a nervous Bower Ismay. In the stables waited the two temperamental sons of Desmond, Craganour and Aboyeur. Around the stands and the marquees were extra police, drafted in to prevent a suffragette demonstration. And in a second-class compartment from Victoria to Tattenham Corner was Emily Davison.

Of them all, Aboyeur had the most eventful journey. A few days before, as he'd done before his only win as a two year old, Cunliffe's colt unseated his work rider at Druid's Lodge and set off down the road to Salisbury. A mightily relieved Tommy Lewis saw him safely back in his stable, but then Aboyeur went lame in his final work before the Derby. A dejected Lewis rode back from Ashburton's convinced that Aboyeur would miss the big race. Surprisingly, the colt walked back sound into the yard. Lewis couldn't get him into the London train fast enough. Advised that all was well with Aboyeur – at least, as well as it ever could be – and that he was safely stabled at Epsom, Cunliffe went to his bank on the morning of the race and drew out £500. He handed it to a commission agent, Walter Fry, and told him to back Aboyeur on the course, each way.

A modern-day bet of £21,500 each way would strike even the highest of high rollers as a serious wager. But by Druid's Lodge's betting standards £250 each way wasn't a large amount. Of the bet, £25 each way was for Purefoy, and just a fiver for Edward Wigan. Despite Purefoy's moans about not being able to strike a decent bet, the Confederates certainly hadn't given up trying. About that time, Tommy Lewis prepared an apparently hopeless case called Hey-Diddle-Diddle for a plunge. Hey-Diddle-Diddle ran all over the place as a two year old, usually in sellers and only once ever placed. Lewis had him fired, gave him one 'easy' at the start of 1913, and got him ready to run for money in a seller at Sandown. Cunliffe and Purefoy motored to Esher in high spirits. The betting forecast was 100–8.

Anticipation turned to outrage when a market formed for Hey-Diddle-Diddle's race. He was 5–4. The top tipster Mark Pizzey had an occasional £5 special wire for his clients. Pizzey didn't bother much with the form book or gallops news. As *London Sketches* explained, "[He] pays handsomely for information, realising it is impossible to obtaining intelligence from the training reports, which are often supplied by the trainers, or persons in their employ." That day, Pizzey's £5 message was short and to the point: 'Hey-Diddle-Diddle? Help yourself.' And they did. Lewis was ordered back to Druid's Lodge to sack the limping 'Shadow' Bishiano, the head lad, who didn't much care. What Pizzey paid him came to two or three years' wages. The inclination to punt was still there. The modesty of the Confederates' bets on Aboyeur simply reflected lack of certainty. Pure was only hopeful, but enough so that plenty of his theatre world cronies had a pound or two each way.

Aboyeur started the Derby at 100–1, having been freely available the day before at double those odds. Up to the Monday he hadn't even got a jockey. Then Edwin Piper became free when another horse was scratched. Piper was hardly a fashionable pilot; his biggest win had been five years previously in the Jubilee. He was retained by George Edwardes, a colourful owner-trainer who managed the Gaiety Theatre for Purefoy. Piper's new mount was one of a trio dismissed in *The Sportsman* as 'far better in their stables than possibly interfering with some of the others.' For *The Sporting Life*, Aboyeur could be 'dismissed from calculations.'

Still, Piper had his tune to play, and the score had been written for him by Cunliffe and Purefoy. He sent Aboyeur straight into the lead from Craganour, Louvois, the French challenger Nimbus and Frank Wootton's mount Shogun. At the first uphill turn Nimbus was knocked sideways by the King's horse Anmer and almost brought down, going from fourth to last in a matter of strides. Aboyeur led by two or three lengths going to the top of the hill, with Craganour closing on him as they began the descent to Tattenham Corner. Day

Comet, Shogun and Louvois led the pursuing group, with Nimbus beginning to make up the ground lost after his mishap. Then as they sighted the turn for home, with Aboyeur still making play from Craganour by a length or a little more, a short middle-aged woman ducked under the rails and wrenched the 1913 Derby for all time from racing lore into the wider arenas of political and social history.

Emily Davison was a brave, determined, single-minded woman – or a vexatious madcap. It depended on one's point of view. Posterity, emancipated, is strongly inclined to the positive verdict. In her own unenlightened times she was regarded, reported and treated as a lunatic. After taking a First at Oxford and spending years in modest obscurity as a teacher, from 1906 Davison devoted herself to the cause of women's suffrage. She made an immediate and spectacular impact. In the years leading up to 1913, she was imprisoned no less than nine times, for obstruction, stone-throwing and setting fire to pillar boxes. On three occasions she was found hiding in the House of Commons, once in a ventilation shaft. She gained early release from prison three times by hunger-striking.

Occasionally the pursuit of her cause had its comic side. One of her prison sentences was for a furious personal assault in Aberdeen on someone she took to be Lloyd George: the shocked old man turned out to be a Scottish Baptist minister. More typical of Davison's lonely crusade were the hunger strikes, the pressure hose turned on her when she barricaded herself in a cell at Strangeways, and what were assumed to be two suicide attempts in June 1912, when she was serving six months in Holloway. Returning to her cell one day, she jumped without warning off the landing and fell onto netting stretched below, specifically to frustrate self-harm. When fished out from the netting by warders, she threw herself down a stone staircase. She later wrote, 'When I attempted to commit suicide I did it deliberately and with all my power because I felt that by nothing but sacrifice of human life would the nation be brought to realise the horrible torture our women face.'

A little after three o'clock on the afternoon of 4 June, Emily Davison was standing against the rails on the inside of Tattenham Corner, wearing a suffragette badge and with two suffragette flags pinned inside her coat. As Reiff on Craganour began his move in pursuit of Aboyeur they galloped towards Davison's place in the crowd. A moment later she slipped under the rails and made a lunge at Aboyeur as he passed her. She made no contact with Aboyeur, or Craganour outside him, or indeed with any of the first nine or ten in the field, most of whom were racing wide of the rails. After the leading group came a gap of several lengths and after the gap, at the head of the three stragglers in the race, came Anmer. Davison, by now right out on the course, only a second or so after Aboyeur had passed her, raised her arms – it seemed to be to snatch at the bridle of the King's horse. She was knocked flying. Anmer was brought down and somersaulted over her. His jockey Herbert Jones was thrown heavily. The two following horses, Jameson and Sandburr, avoided the melee. Anmer was unscathed, and Jones – though severely shaken, concussed and taken to hospital – made a complete recovery, with no more injury than fractured ribs. Davison wasn't so lucky. She lay unconscious after her collision with Anmer, was taken to Epsom Cottage Hospital in a coma and died on the Sunday without ever regaining consciousness.

It was widely thought, and has been repeated endlessly since, that the suffragette had intended to commit suicide, and had thrown herself in front of the King's horse to do so. Neither belief stands up to serious assessment. First, Emily Davison surely didn't commit suicide. An associate was quoted the next day as saying that, 'There is not the slightest doubt that [she] deliberately laid down her life.' The magazine of her movement – *The Suffragette* – ran a memorial issue for her in which it was claimed that 'There can be no doubt that the same conviction [as her attempts in Holloway] led her to make the supreme protest which has resulted in her death.' This was a fragile argument. As a veteran of numerous jail sentences, Davison knew perfectly well – she wasn't blind, after all – that the drop from prison landings was netted. Her leap at Holloway was a protest, as was the tumble downstairs, and the subsequent letter to the Press. This isn't to disparage her courage or sincerity: she was a true believer. But she didn't intend suicide at Holloway, and she certainly didn't intend it at Epsom.

First, she didn't leave a note. The well-established pathology of suicides is that they almost always leave a note. Emily Davison was articulate – an English graduate, a public speaker, a regular writer of magazine articles and letters to Editors – and she was opinionated. She had a cause. Nothing in a horse race could be as certain than that if she'd intended to die at Epsom, she would've left a valedictory message to her fellow suffragettes, to the Press and to the wider world. More prosaically, Emily bought a *return* rail ticket to Tattenham Corner that day. And having arrived at Epsom and joined the crowd, she pencilled the results of the first two races on her race card. That's hardly the state of mind of a would-be suicide. No, she didn't duck under the rails to kill herself; nor did she pick out the King's horse. She was standing against the rails on the inside of the course. This is a crucial point, for she was a short woman and the crowds at race meetings in those days were vastly greater than they are today. As news photographs and film of that day at Epsom show clearly, the crowd inside Tattenham Corner was six to eight – or more – deep. At the back, spectators were standing on benches or carriages. A short woman against the rails, with the crowd behind her, couldn't have seen a single yard of the first mile of the Derby. Only a confusing crescendo of noise would have indicated that the horses were approaching. She had a view of perhaps twenty yards up the sharply curving running rail. She had a grip on the suffragette flags under her coat and had seen the news photographers and the film crews. She was going to jump out in front of the Derby field, unfurl her flags – and make a demonstration public beyond anything she'd achieved before.

What actually happened was that Aboyeur, Craganour and their pursuers were on her before she could react. Hence the lunge towards Aboyeur as he passed. Then, moving as quickly as she could, she jumped out. Faster, far faster than she imagined possible, the horses were passing her. Then on galloped Anmer. She raised an arm in self-defence. After that, oblivion. From where Emily Davison stood, the greatest race-reader born would have been lucky to pick out one horse's colours to lunge at. It was bad luck – not planning – that the King's horse was the one she fell under. It was far worse luck – not suicide – that she paid with her life for her publicity seeking.

14.

An Account Closed

UP FRONT ON Aboyeur and Craganour, Edwin Piper and Johnny Reiff knew nothing of the drama enacted just behind them. In line for home, with Aboyeur on the rails, Reiff sent Craganour up to challenge. As soon as he saw the other horse – the first he'd sighted in the race – Aboyeur lunged sideways to savage him. Piper, strangely for a jockey who already had the advantage of the Epsom rail, had his whip in his left hand and applied it vigorously.

Whether it was flinching from the whip or his continued assault on Craganour, Aboyeur edged steadily out from the rail. Reiff, the last jockey on earth to have it said that he'd met a harder man in a race, got his stick in his right hand and set about straightening Craganour onto the hanging Aboyeur. Close behind, the supreme contemporary rider of Epsom – the apostle of the inside all the way – was poised to pounce. As Aboyeur rolled away from the rails towards Craganour, Frank Wootton gathered Shogun. His supporters in the stands saw Shogun's head poke up inside Aboyeur, and no sooner had their roar gone up than Aboyeur closed the gap. It appeared again, and so did Shogun, but the gap closed once more.

From the furlong pole, Aboyeur hung for every stride onto Craganour, Piper still with his stick in his left hand. He hit Aboyeur 10 times in the last 200 yards. Reiff, his path to a third Derby (he won in 1907 on 'Boss' Croker's Orby and in 1912 on the filly Tagalie) blocked by this persistent and unpleasant challenge, got to the bottom of Craganour. In the last few yards, as onlookers described it, Craganour gave a sort of flying leap over onto Aboyeur, and got his head in front where it mattered.

On the outside of these two exhausted horses, a tremendous challenge had been mounted by Nimbus. The amateur rider, trainer and punter Campbell Russell was based in France in those days. He was convinced that the French three year olds were useless. He jumped in with both feet, turned bookmaker, and laid Nimbus to lose £20,000 (*over £1.7 million*). As he recalled it: 'On the outside, nearest to the grandstand, Nimbus started to come up like a hurricane. That colt seemed to be travelling faster than any horse had ever done before. Each stride brought him nearer and nearer.'

Nimbus, on his knees after two furlongs, was undoubtedly an unlucky loser. But the definitive hard luck story belonged to Great Sport. Going into the last furlong, despite Aboyeur's hanging off the rails and Craganour's efforts to put him back, there was daylight between the two. On Great Sport, George Stern elected to make his challenge between horses. Newsreel film taken from the inside rails by the winning post shows clearly that Great Sport was up with Aboyeur's and Craganour's quarters when the gap closed abruptly. Without any question, the culprit was Aboyeur, diving once more to his right under Piper's left-hand whipping.

On the film, Great Sport's challenge is seen to disappear. A few strides later, though, Craganour is taken off his hind legs, suggesting that Stern has pulled Great Sport sharply to the right, looking for daylight, and has careered into Craganour in doing so. A few strides later still, and Craganour – hampered not just by Aboyeur but by Great Sport also – dives into his principal tormentor as they reach the post. On Craganour's outside now, Great Sport sprints into a place between Craganour and Nimbus. Craganour, Aboyeur, Great Sport and Nimbus pass the post almost in line. At that point, Aboyeur is perhaps the width of six horses off the inside rail. Well inside him comes Louvois, almost level, and inside Louvois is Day Comet, under Judge Robinson's nose.

There's never been a finish to the Derby to compare with 1913, and it's unlikely if there ever will be again. They finished six abreast like a sprint handicap. The excitement and uproar in the stands and on the Downs can be imagined. After an agonised pause, up went Judge Robinson's verdict. Craganour by a head and a neck, from Aboyeur and Louvois, with Great Sport fourth and Nimbus fifth. A colossal shout went up: the favourite had landed the public's gamble.

But even as Reiff was riding Craganour in to be welcomed by Jack Robinson and Bower Ismay, the players were re-forming for the next act of that afternoon's drama. Frank Wootton, who after his unsuccessful pokes up the inside on Shogun had admitted defeat and virtually pulled him up, was on the receiving end of a furious dressing down from Leopold de Rothschild. Had Wootton been anywhere else on the course, Rothschild insisted, he would have won the Derby – and easily. Piper and Cunliffe were head to head. Both knew Aboyeur – bleeding badly from a cut leg – had contributed more than his share to a rough race. Coming down off the stand, Bob Sievier told all in earshot that every jockey in the race should be stood down for a month for dangerous riding. Bad luck on the minority who were innocent, like Maher or the tail-enders, roared Sievier – the only way to be sure of getting all the guilty was to ban the lot. Also hurrying from the stand was Eustace Loder. A friend congratulated him on breeding a Derby winner. 'He has not won it yet,' replied Loder, and rushed on. At about that moment, the jockeys involved in Robinson's assessment of the finish had weighed in. There was a feeling, as well there might be, that an objection could be pending. It was revealed later that Eustace Loder expected Percy Cunliffe to object.

Cunliffe, however, had heard from his jockey that there were no grounds for an objection. Piper was terrified that his mount's role in the scrimmage up the straight would result in his own disqualification. With the jockeys weighed in, and the news rippling round the unsaddling area that Cunliffe wasn't objecting, the Clerk of the Scales had no reason not to give the 'All Right.' It was called, and the flag hoisted.

Eustace Loder had been searching for his fellow stewards, the Lords Rosebery and Wolverton. Incredibly, they watched the race from three different places – Loder from the Jockey Club box, the other two from their respective private boxes – so that in effect they saw three different races. Loder was also frantically trying to find out whether Aboyeur's connections were objecting. On discovering they weren't, he turned prosecutor. The All Right was countermanded. Slowly, the news spread round the enclosures – where bookmakers were already paying out over Craganour – that there was an objection, and that it had been lodged by the stewards themselves. The objection, initiated solely by Loder, was on the grounds that Craganour had 'jostled the second horse.'

Rosebery declared an interest, namely that he had a runner in the race, and though Prue had never remotely threatened involvement, the high-minded Rosebery insisted that he couldn't be part of the steward's enquiry. That left just Wolverton and Loder. The fact that two stewards didn't make a quorum went unnoticed. In the betting ring, 5–1 was offered against Aboyeur getting the race. Not too much need be made of this, for the bookmakers had gigantic liabilities over Craganour – many had virtually a one-horse book –

and almost nothing over Aboyeur. They were glad to get some of the 100–1 chance into their satchels. Prudent favourite backers had an opportunity to hedge. One professional, with a fortune at stake on Craganour, took £5,000 to £1,000 insurance about Aboyeur (£85,900 to win £430,000). His bookmaker later told him he was delighted to pay out: Craganour would have been far more expensive.

The enquiry was no contest. Racecourse stewards combine the roles of judge and jury. At Epsom that day, Loder assumed the role of prosecutor as well. Nor could Craganour hope for any mercy from the selection of witnesses that Loder summoned. One, apparently a decisive contributor, was the judge, Robinson. After the ridicule heaped on him over the 2,000 Guineas result, it would be asking a lot of human nature for him not to have had a touch of anti-Craganour sentiment. And Robinson contrived to underline his incompetence at Epsom. Once again, the horse under his nose – this time Day Comet –went unnoticed. He was placed nowhere by Robinson, yet Day Comet was at worst fourth. Loder called the jockeys into the stewards' room. Saxby, who rode Louvois, was still smarting from his 'jocking off' Craganour. The substance of his evidence can be gauged by the fact that when the eventual result of the enquiry was announced, Saxby waved his hat in the air triumphantly outside the weighing room, for all the world as if he'd won the race himself.

Day Comet's rider Snowy Whalley, who was with or close behind the leaders all the way – and who the stewards were to name as a victim of interference – wasn't called to give evidence. Yet the seventh-placed Wootton was called: Wootton, who was himself suspended more often than any of his contemporaries for rough and reckless riding, and who had the furious criticisms of Shogun's owner fresh in his ears. Wootton's testimony was music to Loder's ears. By the time he'd rehearsed it a few times, it came out fluently for the Press:

Never has Shogun impressed me so, and he literally flew
after making the bend into the home stretch. Half-way down
the straight an opening big enough to take a wagon through
presented itself, and at the instant I pulled my mount into
the gap Aboyeur came rolling towards me. One stride more,
I should have been shut out. My shouts to Piper received the
response that Reiff's mount was causing the pressure and this
seemed plain when I pulled behind them. The same thing
occurred half a furlong further on and after easing my mount
again I could see my chance was hopeless, as the animals on
the outside were so bunched together that it would have been
useless for me to have tried to do any good by pulling out so
far, with the winning post so near.

But as the film of the last furlong shows, there was *still* room for
Wootton to take a wagon through, if he hadn't given up prematurely.
Was it any wonder he looked for a whipping-boy and found the
resented import, Reiff?

Besides Robinson and Wootton, the stewards Loder and
Wolverton called the jockeys on what Robinson had judged to be
the first four horses home: Reiff, Piper, Saxby and Stern. Piper said
as little as he dared. From expecting serious trouble, he found himself
on the brink of being handed the richest prize of his life. Stern picked
up the one-sided tenor of Loder's questioning pretty quickly. When
he emerged from the stewards' room he told a friend conclusively,
'They're going to disqualify that bloody horse.'

Among the mysteries of that extraordinary day was the calling
of the All Right by what the stewards called, without further
explanation, 'an unauthorised person.' Sir Merrik Burrell – who
travelled back from Epsom with Loder that day – gave a strong hint
that the Clerk of the Scales had indeed given the nod. 'I suppose

the Clerk heard that Mr Cunliffe would not object, and the jockeys having weighed in, hoisted the All Right flag without consulting the stewards.'

The Jockey Club rushed to Loder's rescue by decreeing that All Right was inadequate as an indication that jockeys had passed the scales. The *Racing Calendar* carried the instruction to Clerks of the Course that 'The words All Right are not to be used. They may be misleading to the public in the event of an objection being subsequently made.' Any words would be misleading if an objection was made subsequently, but that was perhaps too subtle a point for the Jockey Club. The phrase Weighed In was introduced, and remains to this day.

At Epsom, the minutes passed. The *Daily Express* was emphatic: 'It should definitely be recorded that a flag with the words All Right on it was hoisted on the notice board immediately opposite the grandstand and that it flew there for at least five minutes before it was lowered.' When it came down, it was at the instigation of Lord Durham – 'Determined Jack.' He pushed into the winner's enclosure, looking in Sidney Galtrey's famous phrase 'Rather fierce and terribly serious.' He asked sharply who had given the authority for the All Right? Craganour, by now being led away onto the course, was brought back. At length – another race was run before the enquiry ended – the verdict came.

> The stewards objected to the winner on the grounds that he jostled the second horse. After hearing the evidence of the judge and several of the jockeys riding in the race, they found that Craganour, the winner, did not keep a straight course, and interfered with Shogun, Day Comet and Aboyeur. Having bumped and bored the second horse they disqualified Craganour and awarded the race to Aboyeur.

The announcement caused pandemonium as it spread round the racecourse. Many bookmakers had paid out over Craganour before the objection was called. 'A group of Frenchmen who had backed Craganour entirely declined to understand the situation,' it was reported. The lengthy enquiry disappointed innumerable sweepstake winners. A Wolverhampton hospital surgeon was briefly the holder of the winning ticket in the biggest sweep of those days, the Calcutta – a colossal pot equivalent to *£4 million* or so.

Conversely, there was the City messenger boy whose employer drew Aboyeur in the Stock Exchange sweep. The boy was given the ticket 'for all the good it'll do you' – and collected £1,875 (*£167,800*). The rumour machine spoke at once of a fabulous Druid's Lodge coup. One of the London bookmakers had lost £40,000 and there were long faces elsewhere, it was said. According to one daily paper, 'Aboyeur was extensively backed in the SP offices, and most of the wagers were received by wire between 2.45 and 3.00 pm.' Fanciful stuff, but it *was* a big win – plenty big enough to sprinkle salt on Ladbrokes' tail. Cunliffe's commission agent had picked one of the firm's on-course representatives as the recipient of his £250 each way.

Consternation at Craganour's success had been followed by rapture in the Ladbrokes office when Aboyeur was promoted. The office showed a profit of *£2 million* or so on the race, champagne flowed and a congratulatory telegram was sent round to Cunliffe's rooms. Then the senior Ladbrokes racecourse layer Helen Vernet arrived with the news of Cunliffe's on-course bet. Silence fell. In one stroke, the office profit was wiped out. Furious, Ladbrokes paid Cunliffe the ultimate bookmaker's compliment to a winning punter. His account was closed with immediate effect.

The disqualification raged in the press for some days. Even an Establishment-inclined journalist like Sidney Galtrey felt unable to

shield his *Daily Telegraph* readers from the reality that the stewards'
verdict wasn't universally popular:

> In the endeavour to write honestly and without prejudice,
> it is a duty to say that the disqualification meets with severe
> criticism and condemnation among many whose ideas of
> clean sport are beyond question.

One such critic was Meyrick Good of *The Sporting Life:*

> I have no hesitation in stating that in my opinion Aboyeur
> was the real transgressor. No one had a better view of the race
> than I, and that was my conclusion. Nothing that I have heard
> since has ever induced me to change that view.

Bower Ismay took his appalling reverse over Craganour stoically. There
was talk about an appeal, and plenty of encouragement from his friends
and the Press, but his heart wasn't in it. After the 48 hours allowed for
an appeal, he changed his mind on the grounds that 'The formalities
had not been complied with,' but he didn't pursue the matter. The fact
was that Craganour, who had won two classics and none, had already
been sold to Argentina for £30,000. Ismay made it a condition of the
sale that Craganour should never race again. The Argentine bloodstock
agent told the Press that 'It was very few hours after the Derby was
run that I bought Craganour. Mr Ismay decided to sell because he had
reached the state of mind when he wanted to rid himself of a tragically
unfortunate horse.' The Confederates were also keen to sell. Purefoy
was on the 'phone the following day to the Press and to agents, with a
price tag on Aboyeur of £18,000. There were no takers.

After recovering from his cut leg, Cunliffe's colt ran twice more.
He was third in a £2,000 race at Liverpool, finishing three lengths

behind the second horse, Night Hawk, giving 24lbs. Night Hawk went on to win the St Leger by two lengths. Aboyeur finished with racing in the Gordon Stakes at Goodwood, second when again conceding 24lbs. Purefoy then found a buyer, in the shape of the Imperial Racing Club of St Petersburg. The Russians paid £13,000 for Aboyeur, who was shipped through the Mediterranean to the Crimea. He disappeared after the 1917 revolution. All sorts of stories were told, the most persistent being that he was evacuated with a British military mission to Serbia with a fellow Derby winner, Minoru, the pair last seen between the shafts of a wagon.

A Cunliffe family version has it that with the Bolsheviks destroying anything that smacked of Imperial days, Aboyeur's groom took it on himself to walk the horse from St Petersburg back to the Crimea. The journey took six months. Both horse and groom arrived in a miserable state, but a White Russian officer under the command of General Denikin commandeered Aboyeur and took him for his cavalry charger. Aboyeur's eventful life ended in battle. Craganour fared rather better. He was an outstanding success at stud in Argentina.

Eustace Loder hardly lasted a year. The verdict on him has to be left open. On the one hand, he was known to detest Ismay. His remark before the objection, 'He has not won it yet,' reveals a mind prejudiced if not actually set firm. He conducted an enquiry, on the Derby of all races, without a quorum in the stewards' room and appears to have hand-picked witnesses to support a disqualification. In Loder's defence, it's possible that a modern set of stewards, with head-on and side-on video replays and the advantage that all concerned would at least see the race from the same place, would also disqualify Craganour. But they would surely stand down Aboyeur as well.

Many a horse has drifted down the Epsom camber into the rails opposite the stands. Not a few have caused interference in so doing.

But how many horses with the favoured rails position drift *up* the camber? Especially while – by the stewards' verdict – being bumped and bored by a horse on the outside? If Craganour was responsible, how come he was driven right into the middle of the course? And why was no punishment meted out to Craganour's rider Reiff, who, if the stewards were right, had to be guilty of careless if not dangerous riding? Observers by the winning post were unanimous in naming Aboyeur as, if not the sole offender in what George Stern called more a bull-fight than a horse-race, at least a 50–50 participant. The film evidence is that all through the last furlong he hung badly right, while Craganour ran straight. Aboyeur hampered Great Sport, and should have been disqualified for that if nothing else.

The mitigating circumstance for Loder is that he was already terminally ill with progressive kidney failure, compounded by heart trouble, so his judgement may well have been clouded. He died a year later, wearied by the persisting criticism of his disqualification of Craganour. The tone was set in the papers the day after the Derby in a transparent reference to Loder: 'It was opposed to human nature for one person at Epsom not to exult over the revision of the placings.'

Wilfred Purefoy was oblivious to all the goings-on. He thought so little of Aboyeur's winning chance that early on the morning of Derby day, he could be found buying cattle at Tipperary Fair. "By the time I caught the train to Dublin I was tired and slept peacefully." At Maryborough an excited guard woke him and said, 'Your honour, Aboyeur was second.' "Thank God! I exclaimed and went to sleep again. When the train arrived at Kingsbridge, Mr Smyth, the courteous superintendent of the line, came to meet me and said Aboyeur had got the race. Unfortunately, I caught sight of Mr Peard waiting for me in his motor, and thought it was one of his celebrated practical jokes. I was inclined to be peevish, and I would not believe it till I saw it in the evening papers."

Not for the first time, the 1913 Derby gave Cunliffe the chance to show off his supreme cynicism. 'AP' had a stupendous win over Aboyeur. Together with his £2 *million* swipe at Ladbrokes, his little 'fun' bets on Aboyeur during the preceding winter added up to the biggest win of his life, Hackler's Pride included. In later years, he produced his betting book to prove the point. Yet when his chauffeur drove him down to Druid's Lodge, past gallops poles festooned with flags, Cunliffe just grunted gloomily: 'What silly bugger's put those up?' But the staff all got a bonus of two weeks' wages, and Aboyeur's long-suffering lad Hughie Murphy was rewarded with £25. Later, Cunliffe – hardly a pauper before the Derby, and certainly not after it – had a suggestion for Wigan. 'You're a rich man, Ted. Why don't you take the pot, and I'll take the prize money?' So the gold trophy went back with Wigan to Conholt Park. There it stayed for 75 years until a robbery in January 1988. Despite a reconstruction of the theft on the BBC's *Crimewatch*, the trophy, commemorating the most eventful Derby of all, has still to be recovered.

15.

Breaking Even

THE KAISER ACCOMPLISHED what the handicapper, the Jockey Club and the bookmakers could not. The 1914–18 war brought about the end of the Confederacy. Druid's Lodge was requisitioned, and troops manoeuvred on the gallops. Most of the lads volunteered or were called up, and racing was reduced to a level where the prize-money available couldn't sustain the expense of a large stable. When the war ended, there was little chance of bringing the Confederates back together. It was 22 years since they first gathered together on Salisbury Plain. They'd been young men then. Now, they were approaching late middle age. They'd been rich: they were still wealthy, but the fat in their incomes had melted away in the war, especially for those like Wigan who had large foreign investments.

Cunliffe patched up the gallops. Very soon, he'd send out an Oaks winner from Druid's Lodge. But as the country and the racing community slowly returned to peacetime, there was no prospect of the Confederacy re-forming. The stables at Druid's Lodge had been closed when Cunliffe sold them to James (JV) Rank in 1934. The yard had first been offered to Steve Donoghue for £18,000 – a fraction of what Cunliffe had spent there; but Donoghue decided it was too remote for his start as a trainer.

Rank was one of a pair of entrepreneurial brothers who left a significant mark on British industry. 'JV' was a miller whose firm became Rank Hovis McDougall. His brother J. Arthur was the pre-eminent film-maker of his day, and founded the Rank Organisation. JV asked his brother if the history of Druid's Lodge would make an interesting movie? No, replied J. Arthur, he'd just made a film about racing, based on Edgar Wallace's *The Calendar*, and that was enough for the moment. In some ways JV Rank was a surprising racehorse owner and successor to Percy Cunliffe. He was a Quaker who didn't bet, but that didn't stop him investing as heavily as Cunliffe, building a second yard at the back of the original stables.

In 1935, Rank installed Noel Cannon as his flat race trainer, with Gwyn Evans to train a few jumpers. Evans was killed soon after in a motor accident on his way back from Newbury races, but Cannon brought fresh lustre to Druid's Lodge. His first good horse was Scottish Union, who won the 1938 St Leger after seconds in both the 2,000 Guineas and Derby. In the substitute 1943 Oaks, he saddled the winner Why Hurry. During the war Rank, who was as keen on coursing as on thoroughbreds, staged pre-Waterloo Cup meetings at Druid's Lodge. Cannon's other big-race wins for Rank included the 1949 Cesarewitch with Strathspey and the 1950 Hunt Cup with Hyperbole. He brought Scobie Breasley to England in 1950 to be the stable's first jockey. Years after, the man from Wagga Wagga recalled with horror the cold mornings riding work on Salisbury Plain. 'You just pile on extra clothes and hope that you'll get used to it in due course. You never do.'

Breasley rode with success and distinction for Cannon during 1950 and 1951, but progressively fell out with Rank's wife Pat – a gigantic punter, in contrast to her husband – and returned to Australia. The following year, Rank died, and his executors sold Druid's Lodge to Jack Olding, the tractor manufacturer and motor trader. Olding paid £200,000 for the estate. He in turn passed the stables on to the whisky magnate James Dewar, and before long Cannon sent out Festoon to win the 1954 1,000 Guineas in Dewar's colours, ridden by Scobie Breasley. That August, Dewar died. Druid's Lodge was sold to a farming company, and its gallops were ploughed up to plant potatoes.

In the summer of 1989, the 3,333-acre estate was put on the market by its owners, Drucella Farming. Many racing trainers and owners asked about Druid's Lodge, but the agents advised them that the gallops would take years to restore. The estate was sold to a Sussex landowner, Robert Hurst, for £12.5 million. The following year, he applied for planning permission to build a 120-bedroom hotel, conference centre and two golf courses at Druid's Lodge. The plan was approved, but mercifully never implemented, and in 1992 he sold the estate for a reported £10 million to the late Elisabeth, Lady Moyne, and other members of the Guinness family. Thoughts of commercial development were shelved: "We're serious farmers," said Lady Moyne at the time.

During the 1980s the old yard was let to a livery and competition yard run by Sorrel Warwick. Cunliffe and Rank had built so well that when she moved in, the stables – empty for over 30 years – needed 'nothing more than dusting down and brushing out.' Warwick used the yard to break and school horses for local owners and trainers, and to prepare event horses and riders. Spain's eventing team spent several months at Druid's Lodge in preparation for the Seoul Olympics.

Since June 1994, the yard has been at the heart of Giles and Tae Ormerod's Druid's Lodge Polo. School and University polo teams go to Druid's Lodge for coaching. The facilities include five grass polo fields and a floodlight arena. There's a circular all-weather canter, build over a sand ring that Cunliffe installed for Jack Fallon. The dormitories where the Confederates' lads and apprentices were locked up, playing German Banker and fighting each other, have been divided into grooms' single rooms. And horses' heads still look out from the boxes that housed Ypsilanti and Hackler's Pride and Lally and Christmas Daisy and Aboyeur. The broader estate, apart from the gallops, is intact from Percy Cunliffe's day. Besides the polo and a commercial shoot, the land is given over to arable crops and a dairy farm.

The Confederates never made the same mark as individuals that they had as a team. For their employees Jack Fallon and Ben Dillon, the fortunes brought to them by their association with Cunliffe and Purefoy were quickly scattered. Jack hugely enjoyed the opportunities to show off his wealth. When he went back to Roscommon to visit his relatives, he travelled in style in a fancy carriage. He threw extravagant parties. In London too, he did far more carousing and card-playing than was good for his new role as a public trainer. Plenty of owners wanted a touch of the Druid's Lodge magic applied to their horses, and they happily patronised Jack's yard at Winterbourne Stoke. Among them were Ambrose Gorham, the shrewd insurance clerk turned big-league bookmaker; the cattle barons Sir William Nelson and Joe Shepherd; and the German Baron Richthofen. But without the restraining hand of Purefoy and the patience of Cunliffe, Fallon was nothing. He landed a big coup for Gorham in the 1911 Manchester handicap with Ultimus, and that was the best he had to show for several years' training in his own right. He knew nothing about agriculture, and his farms soaked up money unstoppably. He knew even less about people. Every sharp in London was at his side in an instant, taking his money and touting him bad horses. The last straw came when he backed a large bill for Derrick Wernher, the seemingly wealthy son of a prominent family. Fallon found himself having to stump up for that and other defaults, and within five years pretty well everything he had was sold up and gone. By the end of 1911 he was firmly in the grip of the moneylenders, borrowing sums like £500 with interest of £250 over three months. Scotland Lodge was sold, and for a while one of his owners installed him at Elston Lodge, the yard in Shrewton where Bob Sievier trained before him and Steve Donoghue after.

By 1917, Jack had become so desperate that he went to the King's Bench to claim conspiracy against the numerous moneylenders who were hounding him. He alleged that they'd worked in league to lend him an ever-increasing spiral of money to pay off each other's debts and interest. Some familiar names – Parson Parkes, 'Boss' Croker – cropped up in a sad and complicated story of failed gambles and bad debts. Jack never spoke a truer word than when he admitted in court, 'I am not very much up in figures.' The case was withdrawn after three days of hearings. Jack won a reprieve from the moneylenders, who for their part realised he had nothing left to give them. He'd squandered the accumulated fortune of his Druid's Lodge successes at something like £800,000 a year. He drifted back to Ireland during the war. Afterwards his luck seemed to have taken a turn for the good when he was called by the financier Jimmy White to his offices in the Strand. White was in the process of setting up a stable of all the talents at Foxhill, near Swindon. He installed Martin Hartigan as his private trainer, settled all Jack's debts, gave him a stern warning about drinking and card-playing, and made him Hartigan's assistant and head lad.

Steve Donoghue was the stable jockey. Among the lads at the start of 1920 was a tiny 15-year-old called Gordon Richards. Some good gambles were landed, but White was far too erratic an owner to leave his professional stable team alone. He liked nothing more than to motor down from London on a Sunday with his retinue of hangers-on and have all his horses paraded. Sometimes he insisted on having them galloped, deaf to the pleadings of Hartigan and Fallon that they'd all been worked the day before. He had a notion, gleaned from the *crayères* of the Reims region, that champagne tasted better if it was stored in chalk, so Jack and the lads were forever excavating the downs to store White's bubbly. As like as not, it all had to be dug up again the following Sunday. White's empire unravelled in 1927, taking with it the savings of many of his racing friends and confidants, Steve Donoghue among them. White poisoned himself, and the Foxhill stable and a stud of 60 or 70 brood mares were sold as part of the dispersal to pay his creditors.

Jack had split with White long before his suicide. 'White knew nothing whatever about horses, and would listen to the advice of anybody but his trainer. Instead of doing my job I was constantly preparing Foxhill for visitors.' He tried to set up as a trainer at Epsom but no one was interested. He drifted around the fringes, helping out at Herbert Smyth's and with the actor-trainer Tom Walls, and saddling a couple for the Manton trainer, Alec Taylor. All the while, everything that he still possessed was hocked or sold, even minor personal souvenirs like a presentation photograph album of Ambrose Gorham's horses at Scotland Lodge – 'popped' to the landlord of the Victoria at Shrivenham. The most that racing regulars saw of Jack by now was cadging for a pound or two at racecourse entrances. It upset many of them, and in April 1935 Steve Donoghue, Herbert Smyth, Meyrick Good and others organised a fund for Jack through the pages of the *Life*. The affection for Jack that still ran right across the racing community was shown by the fund's contributors. Arthur Bendir of Ladbrokes gave a tenner. So, ironically, did Sir George Thursby, the rider of second-placed Picton in Lally's disastrous Derby. Another bookmaker, Daniel Gant, chipped in as did Lord Howard de Walden and the Earls of Lonsdale and Huntingdon. Appeal cards were posted up at Epsom during the Derby meeting, and collection boxes rattled there all week.

Jack died the following year, the fund having at least provided something for his widow Blanche and their children Margaret, John and Nina. He was buried in North London by his friend Father John Caulfield, the 'jockeys' priest' who ran a charity donkey derby on the Sunday after Epsom each year, patronised by Steve Donoghue and other top riders. Father John used to say optimistically that 'Jockeys are all very good fellows.' He was a kind man, and he wrote to Nina Fallon to say, 'I prized [Jack's] friendship very highly for so many years. The world would be better for more men such as John Fallon. He was big hearted and generous to a fault.'

The Sporting Life had no doubts about Jack's standing. It led the front page with the news of his death, headlined: *Trainer-Genius of Druid's Lodge*. 'No trainer that we can recall made fewer mistakes than did Fallon during the period he was master at Druid's Lodge.' Some old friends were at Jack's funeral, Ben Dillon and Alec Taylor among them. None of the surviving Confederates was there, though it is as sure as anything can be that his old mentor Wilfred Purefoy would have attended. But by then, Pure himself was dead. What a rollercoaster ride Jack had through life. From a smallholding in Roscommon to lording it over his own lands, then down to cadging for charity at the same places where once every hand clapped his back and every ear was bent to his advice. He left a fractured family behind him. His eldest daughter married at 19 and emigrated to Australia; she and her father never saw each other again. His son John had finished his first year at a Catholic public school when the bailiffs moved against his father. He disappeared from the school's register and later cut himself off completely from his father and the rest of the family.

Poor Jack. Poor Bernard, too. Dillon's downfall was every bit as swift. He had a few short years at the top of his profession. He

rode Pretty Polly to her last four victories, and won the 1906 1,000
Guineas on Flair, as well as that year's Grand Prix on Spearmint.
He won the 1,000 again in 1909 on Electra, and then the Derby the
following year on Lemberg. It was his last big win. He had ever-
worsening weight problems, and he was betting unsuccessfully. His
career as a jockey came to an abrupt end. In an act of indescribable
folly, a small-time owner-trainer called George Aston took him to
court in 1913 to claim £660 that Dillon owed him from some failed
gambles. 'Dillon employed me to bet for him,' Aston told the judge,
who pretty smartly ruled that betting disputes were no business of
his court. But the damage had been done: the Jockey Club warned
off both Aston and Dillon.

By then, though, Dillon seemed to have found a second meal
ticket. In 1907 he had been an usher at the wedding of a fellow
jockey. Among the bridesmaids was the music hall star Marie
Lloyd. She was married, and almost 20 years Ben's senior, but that
didn't stop them forming a long-standing relationship. After he'd
been warned off, he accompanied Marie on a tour of America. She
travelled openly as Mrs Dillon. The authorities took a different view
of such arrangements in those days, and for a while the immigration
authorities on New York's Ellis Island locked them up for immoral
behaviour. Eventually, word came through that her second husband
had died, and she married Ben in Oregon. Back home, she was soon
complaining that he was knocking her about. His standing in the
racing world never recovered from his lending his name to a get-
rich-quick tipping service. In 1922 Marie died. It was said 50,000
lined the streets to see her hearse go by. Dillon rode alone in a cab,
watched in silence by Marie's worshipping fans.

History hasn't been kind to Ben, at least that version put about by
show business sentimentalists. But Marie Lloyd was a spender well
up to classic standard. However much she earned, and in her prime

it was plenty, she spent or gave it away. Her family was curiously entwined with racing. One of her sisters married a trainer, another the jockey 'Whip' Wheatley. Two nieces married jockeys – George Duller and Charlie Smirke – and her daughter by her first husband married another, Tubby Ayling. Her first two husbands were both losing punters, and so was she. By the time of her death Marie and Ben were living in a house in Golders Green bought for them by her sisters, on their charity. Ben spent the rest of his life in obscurity, dying in 1945 at the early age of 54. The rider of Spearmint and Pretty Polly ended his days as a night porter in Trafalgar Square.

In contrast to the miserable endings of Fallon and Dillon, the Confederates died well off. Purefoy made some serious inroads into his profits from the Druid's Lodge years. According to one of his obituaries, 'When he lost the guidance of Mr Cunliffe, his speculative ventures more often than not went awry, and it is understood that he lost a good deal of money.' He acted for some time as racing manager for Arthur Bendir, the founder of Ladbrokes. It seemed an unlikely poacher-and-gamekeeper alliance. Bendir had unhappy memories of the Druid's Lodge coups, not least Aboyeur. But the two became friends after Bendir married one of the girls from Purefoy's Gaiety Theatre. Bendir's horses were trained at what Pure hoped would be a smaller-scale reincarnation of Druid's Lodge. The stable was his original yard at Everleigh. The trainer was one of the Druid's Lodge head lads, Edward Harper.

Together Bendir and Purefoy were involved in one of the liveliest racing scandals of the 1920s, when Mrs Bendir's horse Condover ran poorly in the 1924 Lincoln. It was well fancied. The connections stood to win £34,000 (£1.5 *million*) in bets, £10,000 of that earmarked for Purefoy, who cancelled a New Year visit to America to supervise Condover's preparation. The jockey Rufus Beasley was on a win bonus of £1,000. The horse still ran badly. He then appeared in the Newbury Spring Cup, was backed from 100–7 to 4–1 and won rather easily. The *Evening News* made the obvious imputation:

> Public betting is not the haphazard thing that it used to be –
> the man in the street is by way of being an expert – but when
> he is palpably out-witted and finds all his logical conclusions
> unexpectedly scuttled, he is inclined to think that the game is
> not so nice as it ought to be.

This was tame stuff compared to the things they used to write about Druid's Lodge in the pages of *The Winning Post* and elsewhere, but Margot Bendir sued the *Evening News* for libel and Pure felt obliged to follow suit. They won, but the jury awarded them the derisory damages of one farthing, and their costs were heavy. Edward Harper said that Pure had fatally weakened the cause of Condover's connections by more or less agreeing in the witness box that the newspaper's remarks weren't terribly serious.

In his later years, Pure maintained that he was less and less interested in racing, but still enthralled by breeding. None the less, he was a paddock regular up to the time of his death in 1930. His passing in his rooms in Jermyn Street, above the Turkish baths where he used to keep a beady eye on Ben Dillon while picking the other jockeys' brains, produced more than the usual round of polite regrets. The local newspaper in Tipperary saluted him:

> His employees will miss him sadly. Many of them have grown
> grey in his service. Some have been pensioned but all will
> mourn the passing of a kindly master. The old tenants and
> their successors will also grieve for they recall his fine qualities
> as a landlord. The poor, too, will miss his generous hand.

As practical as you'd expect of a country paper, it also recalled his loan of free services from his prize bulls and his lesser stallions, to help local farmers improve their stock.

Pure left fond memories and an odd request: that his doctor should sever his spinal chord (shades of Charles I) after he was certified dead. He remembered all his staff generously; old Anne, the motherly housekeeper who sat all the stable lads round the kitchen table at Greenfields, was willed £3 a week for life, and every employee was given what amounted to a year's severance. Even his brother's mistresses were beneficiaries. Pure liked to play the simple country boy. He wrote that he could think of nothing nicer than a fishing holiday in Norway or the West of Ireland with 'a dear little soul,' his euphemism for an actress. Yet he was a high-risk entrepreneur, an enthusiastic amateur journalist who wrote as knowledgeably about politics and wildlife as about racing, and the schemer behind some of the biggest gambles on the English turf. He left a depleted estate amounting to £45,074 (over *£2.2 million*).

Holmer Peard lived to the grand age of 86. When the Confederates went their ways at the start of the first world war, he did some training on his own account, the highlight being a Leopardstown Chase winner in 1917. That year his responsibilities at Cork Park ended, when the course was sold for the land to be turned over to motor car manufacture. Peard continued as one of Ireland's major bloodstock agents, investors, dealers and managers into his old age. The Phoenix Park flourished under his direction, and he was in charge there till handing over to his son Harry – the initiator of evening meetings and inventor of the Peard starting gate. For many years after Holmer's death in 1939 there were Peards and Purefoys among the shareholders at the Phoenix Park. Holmer Peard left almost £29,000 (*£1.4 million*), a fortune accumulated entirely from his successful speculations in horseflesh.

Edward Wigan, Percy Cunliffe and Frank Forester all died in 1942. Wigan continued his anonymous lifestyle. He had horses in training with Sandy Braime at Marlborough for a number of years, his last winners coming in 1935. All in all, and including the shared Confederacy horses that ran in his name, he owned the winners of 138 races. Wigan used to hold what he thought were private telephone conversations with Braime about his 'betting cowps' as he mistakenly pronounced them. He constructed a sort of soundproofed booth for these calls; but his wife, as tall and talkative as he was short and silent, found a way of listening at the back, so that all the estate staff at Conholt had their half-crowns on when the guv'nor had a cowp planned. Wigan left the considerable fortune of £412,727 (£15 *million*, even at the depleted values of wartime money).

Percy Cunliffe tried to revive Druid's Lodge after 1918, and he had a handful of horses in training there with Braime in the early 1920s. One was Charlebelle, who revived all sorts of memories of the great days at Druid's Lodge. She was bred at Purefoy's Greenfields, by Charles O'Malley out of Bushey Belle, the winner of that long-ago Curragh maiden race where Hackler's Pride finished second. Charlebelle won the 1920 Oaks for Cunliffe. He was free with the opinion beforehand that the balance of her form wasn't up to classic standard, but that didn't prevent a gamble on the day of the race from 5–1 down to 7–2 second favourite. She won by a hard-fought neck, just getting up in the last few yards to outstay the 1,000 Guineas winner and favourite, Cirra.

As a four year old, Charlebelle featured in a Cesarewitch which was extraordinary for providing Frank Forester with a 100–1 winner – making him surely the only owner to have been associated with 100–1 successes in two major races. Forester's winner was Light Dragoon, whose form suggested not only that he was useless but that he didn't stay. He was a grandson of Forester's controversial Wokingham

winner Queen's Holiday. Charlebelle, despite coughing a week before
the race, was a heavily backed favourite. She ran eleventh, while
Light Dragoon sailed in comfortably, neither Forester nor his trainer
Harper having thought it worth bothering to go to Newmarket.
Cunliffe, wrote the *Daily Graphic*, 'Has an impassive face, but it was
a study in stupefaction after the race,' and no wonder. He did well,
though, from Charlebelle. She was sold to America with her first foal
for 12,000 guineas.

Cunliffe's last winner as an owner was in 1931. He went out with
a bang, albeit a carefully muffled bang. It isn't known who his last
private trainer was – or head lad, since Cunliffe had his own name
on the licence, but between them they sent a four year old called
Claddagh Ring to Hurst Park on the May Bank Holiday, for the
Eel Pie selling plate. The horse had no measurable form, including
when last of 11 in a Kempton seller on its final outing as a three year
old. Claddagh Ring made its seasonal debut at Hurst Park, and not
surprisingly was joint eighth in the betting at 100–8. The surprise was
that it 'Made practically all the running and won by a length.' In one
of the last issues of the *Winning Post*, Bob Sievier wrote a nostalgic
tribute:

> A bank holiday SP job was bought off by Mr AP Cunliffe,
> one of the old Druid's Lodgers, when his Claddagh Ring
> won at Hurst Park. The winner was bought in for 450 guineas,
> which is prodigally in advance of the gelding's value on earlier
> form. Cunliffe used to be co-reigning governor of Druid's
> Lodge with the late Wilfred Purefoy. They bought off more
> betting coups than any other stable.

Percy Cunliffe had 141 winners all told. He and Frank Forester,
the last surviving Confederates, died within a week of each other

in September 1942. Forester had enjoyed himself hugely with the
Quorn during the war. The hunt staff were called up, most of the
horses were requisitioned, and it became harder and harder to find
food for the hounds. Subscriptions dwindled to nothing. But at least
Forester was able to hunt the pack himself and do as he pleased. At
the end of the 1918 season he resigned as Master, pleading fatigue,
having as he put it carried on 'single-handed with my very young
daughter.' The alternative explanation for his decision to leave was
that there was quite a prejudice at that time against a Master acting
as his own huntsman, and with the end of the war in sight Forester
didn't want a huntsman foisted on him. At all events, *Baily's* recorded
that during the harsh times of the war Forester had been 'very
successful in keeping down foxes,' and he continued to hunt with the
Quorn until he became Master of the Wilton in 1927. He had a bad
fall the following year when he was 68, breaking an arm and a leg,
which finally finished his riding. He lived always in supreme style.
When the first of his daughters was married, no less than 400 guests
sat down to lunch. Another 600 farmers and their wives from the
Quorn country were entertained in an adjacent marquee.

Forester's lifetime tally of winners was similar to Wigan's and
Cunliffe's: 125, the majority of them home-bred. Light Dragoon's
Cesarewitch was his last big race. He remained particularly close
to Wigan, and to Purefoy until Pure's death. In old age, Forester
reverted somewhat to the mischief of his youthful escapades with
Purefoy. He liked to teach his grandchildren irritating table manners,
and took particular relish in getting his chef tipsy with a ferocious
punch concocted in a Cleveland family gold bowl. When he was
dying, he lay propped up in bed with a parrot on his shoulder, driving
his solicitor to distraction with repeated changes to his will, and
summoning his nurse from the next room with a toot on a hunting
horn. He specified that his remains should be 'cremated and the ashes

scattered to the four winds.' So they were, on the land at Druid's Lodge where he and the Confederates had watched all those secret gallops years before.

A dinner guest once plucked up the courage to ask Frank Forester how had the books balanced at Druid's Lodge? The old huntsman's eyes gleamed as he thought for a moment of his friends; of their huge outgoings at Druid's Lodge and in bloodstock; of their 400-odd winners; of Fallon and Dillon; of the four Cambridgeshires, the Lincoln, the Wokingham, the Hunt Cup, the two Jubilees, the Eclipse, finally the Derby; of the great gambles lost and landed.

'We about broke even,' Forester chuckled. 'We about broke even.'

Bibliography

BOOKS

Allison, William *Memories of Men and Horses* (1922)

Brown, Frank *Sport from Within* (1952)

Browne, T. H. *History of the English Turf* (1931)

Captain X. *Tales of the Turf* (c. 1944)

Dey, Thomas Henry *Leaves from a Bookmaker's Book* (1910)

Donoghue, Stephen *Just My Story* (1923)

Ellis, Colin *Leicestershire and the Quorn Hunt* (1951)

Felstead, S. Theodore *Racing Romance* (1949)

——*In Search of Sensation*

Galtrey, Sidney *Memoirs of a Racing Journalist* (1934)

Good, Meyrick *Good Days* (1941)

——*The Lure of the Turf* (1957)

Jacob, Naomi *Our Marie*

Jarvis, Jack *They're Off* (1969)

Lambton, George *Men and Horses I have Known* (1924)

Luckman, A. Dick *Sharps, Flats, Gamblers and Racehorses* (1914)

McGuigan, John *A Trainer's Memories* (1946)

Mortimer, Roger *The History of The Derby Stakes* (1962)

——(and others) *Biographical Encyclopaedia of British Flat Racing*

Morton, Charles *My Sixty Years of the Turf* (c. 1930)

Plumptre, George *The Fast Set* (1985)

Poole, Christopher *Scobie* (1984)

Porter, John *John Porter of Kingsclere* (1919)

Russell, Campbell *Triumphs and Tragedies* (1925)

Sarl, Arthur J. *Gamblers of the Turf* (1938)

——*Horses, Jockeys and Crooks* (1935)

Seth-Smith, Michael *Steve* (1974)

Sievier, Robert Standish *Autobiography* (1906)

Simpson, Charles *Leicestershire and its Hunts* (1926)

Sloan, Tod *Tod Sloan by Himself* (1915)

Tanner, Michael *Pretty Polly* (1987)

Todd, Bob *My Racing Memories* (1947)

Welcome, John *Neck or Nothing* (1970)

——*Irish Horseracing* (1982)

——*Infamous Occasions*

British Film Institute *The Derby 1913* [Ref. 602762A]

NEWSPAPERS AND PERIODICALS

Andover Advertiser

Bloodstock Breeders' Review

Cope's Racegoer's Encyclopaedia

Daily Graphic

Daily Mail

Daily Telegraph

Evening News

The Field

Horse and Hound

Illustrated Sporting and Dramatic News

Irish Field

London Sketches

Manchester Evening News

News of the World

The People

Racing Calendar

Reynolds News

The Sporting Life

Sporting Luck

Sporting Sketches
The Sportsman
The Sunday Times
The Tatler
Timeform Chasers and Hurdlers
The Times
The Tipperary Star
Truth
Vanity Fair
The Winning Post

Index